*To:*_____

*From:*_____

*Date:*_____

THE ANCESTORS:

FREEDOM FROM EPIGENETICS AND GENETIC INHERITANCE

Published by
LAC Publications
Rights Reserved

© 2020 LAC Publication
Originally published 2018 in Spanish with the title
"The Ancestor" (The Liberation of Genetic and Epigenetic)
by LAC Publications
© 2020 Mario H. Rivera and Luz Rivera
All rights reserved

ISBN 978-1-735-27442-3

© Mario H. Rivera and Luz Rivera
All rights reserved

No portion of this work may be reproduced, or stored in an information storage system, or transmitted in any medium (electronic, mechanical, photocopying, recording, etc.), without the prior permission of the Publisher. The only exception is shortly citation in printed reviews.

Translated by: Violeta Rivera.(violetrivera@live.com)
Cover Design: Juan Luque
Printed in U.S.A.
Category: Spiritual Warfare

Index

CHAPTER 1
THE EXPERT MINISTRY OF THE SOUL
- What is the ministration of the soul?
- What are the requirements of someone in the area of deliverance?
- Which gifts operate in a deliverance?
- Which are the spirits that attack men and women most frequently?
- How to end a deliverance?
- How does a deliverance team operate?
- The ministration of the soul
- What is not a ministration of the soul?
- Ministration and the present
- A good ministration ensures a good deliverance
- The bible, science, and the genetics
- Genetic heritage
- Ancestors
- Generational weaknesses

CHAPTER 2
THE GENETIC OF THE METAMORPHOSIS
- Regeneration
- The genetic battle
- Orthodox guide of ancestors
- Beyond genetics: the ancestors
- Defending epigenetics
- Noah's perfect genes
- Biblical example of epigenetics
- The science of the epigenetics

CHAPTER 3
THE INTERNAL GENETIC BATTLE
- What is perfection?
- The genealogical line

- The blood bond
- The golgi apparatus
- The golgi complex
- The epigenetic contaminations
- How to break epigenetics
- The DNA repair
- About unequal yoke
- Breaking epigenetics
- What does memory mean?

CHAPTER 4
THE TRANSFORMATION
- The ghost in genetics
- David's genetic ghost
- The epigenetic behavior and destiny
- The genetic repair by excision
- The dna's metamorphosis
- Genetics changed by food

CHAPTER 5
GOD'S (YHWH) GENETICS AND ENGINEERING
- The new breed
- We live for the next generation
- The golgi apparatus part 2
- Golgi: the generational source of information
- Parents' iniquity
- Transferable engineering
- Some of the things that can be found in genetics
- Nutrition and diet that change genetics
- Genetics destiny
- The slave's food
- Biochemical alteration
- Appetites that affect spiritually
- Childhood traumas
- Traumas
- Genetic transformers

- How to break epigenetics?
- The breaking of epigenetics
- Other ways of breaking inherited epigenetics

CHAPTER 6
THE RECEPTORS OF THE GENERATIONAL SPIRIT

- Receptors
- Times of contamination with receivers
- The dynamics between the receptor and transmitter spirit
- Supervision times
- Visitors from two spiritual realms
- God designed us with dna
- Transferable engineering part 2
- Conception
- Genetic battle part 2
- Generational spirit
- Family tree of 14 people
- The ancestors of "the Herods"
- The fourth herodian generation
- Kennedys' ancestors
- Ancestors of Israelite patriarchs'
- David's ancestors
- Cycles of generational spirits
- 7 types of generational spirits

FOREWORD

Genetics is a biological branch that studies the transmission of physical and physiological characteristics and behaviors from one generation to another. This science is considered to be born in 1866 when Australian Monk Gregor Mendel describes basic genetic laws in his study. Unfortunately, it was not until XX century that these laws were accepted by the science community and was then known as "Mendel's Rediscovery." In 1909 "hereditary factors," once described by Mendel came to be known as "genes" by Wilhelm Johansen and later it was discovered that these same genes are physical materials that can be found in the nucleus of cells. As advances in cytology and microbiology occurred, in the year 1940 it is revealed that genes are made of deoxyribonucleic acid (DNA). In the 1950s it is discovered how the DNA molecule is made and in the 1970s, scientists discover how to cut and paste DNA fragments giving birth to genetic engineering. The years that followed mark significant advances in the history of medicine, since the 1980's genes began to be associated with diseases. In 1990 the Human Genome Project began, an investigation carried out by international scientists in which one of the purposes was to identify and locate all the genes in the human genome. It was considered completed in April 2003 and opened the understanding of many diseases by providing tools for diagnosing and for treatment. One example is the contribution to the development of targeted treatments against infectious diseases, cancers, and has helped to gain a better understanding of how certain drugs work. Aside from this, it also brought advances in other science branches reaching agriculture.

It is difficult to summarize in a few words the history or the importance of this science. What we can see is that it has developed over a century and a half and that the discoveries in this area continue. Every day we find new ways genetics are a contributing factor in the process of diseases.

An important detail about this book is that for God's people, the study of genetics is not something that began in the 19th century. In light of the Word we will see that in ancient times it was known that the experiences of the ancestors in one way or another had an impact on the lives of people. As we read Job 8: 8 we see:

Ask, I beg you, past generations, and consider things scrutinized by your parents.

This is a dialog among Bildad and Job. Bildad is trying to console Job and in helping find answers to the grand question: Why am I passing this trial? In the original, Bildad tells Job to ask the "lineage and past generations" and "pay attention to your parents' experiences." Then it continues in verse 9:

For we were born yesterday and know nothing; our days on earth are but a shadow.

For we are but of yesterday, and know nothing, because our days upon earth are a shadow.
"We are but of yesterday and know nothing." Physically we are a product of a mixture of genetic material from our ancestors. Science has taught us that we have inherited physical characteristics from our ancestors but in the Bible, we see that we have a spiritual inheritance. Many of the circumstances that we deal with are

the product of our parents' experiences that many times were hidden from us.

Verse 10 says the following:
Will they not instruct you and tell you? Will they not bring forth words from their understanding?

In researching our generations or lineage, we find instruction, direction, and word. In this book we will find the tools that with help from the Holy Spirit we may investigate and scrutinize our generations and this way find direction and instruction to diagnose and treat problems. I invite you alongside the Apostolic teaching and the Holy Spirit's anointing you may search your spiritual genome and locate each part of your genetic that needs repair. You will see in this book that genetic engineering is not something that started in the 20th century but it started when the son of God shed his precious blood so that we would be new creatures with new genetics. We are a chosen lineage. 1 Peter 2: 9. Amen.

Dr. Mario Rivera is an Apostle, Teacher and Pastor who in his ministerial work has developed his calling in spiritual warfare, deliverance and has published many books, sharing the revelation and wisdom that he has received from the Holy Spirit for the edification of the church.

It is through this books that the body of Christ receive the necessary tools for our battle against darkness and ancestral curses. In fulfilling the call of our God, the Apostle has devoted himself to the study of a branch of genetics not known to science, but which existed long before 1866 when Mendel began to describe the basic principles of genetics. I am talking about divine genetic. The Holy Spirit has revealed to the Apostle that by studying our spiritual genetics, we will have useful tools for the diagnosis, treatment and prevention of diseases, struggles, chains, ties and ancient curses.

As in his previous books, we can expect from this book, a book based on the word of God, inspired by the Holy Spirit to bring glory to Jesus Christ.

Personally, I've known Apostle Mario for over two years. His PhD is in theological science, but his studies have given him a deeper understanding in medicine areas such as semiology, and molecular biology. When I hear him speaking about science, medicine, and the word of God, I have been able to understand that he is a true doctor. The word doctor comes from a Latin root that means teacher or the one who teaches. Apostle Rivera is a teacher of the word that the Lord has used and will keep on using greatly.

My prayer is that, through this book, the Holy Spirit will bring revelation, discernment, and a special training to be prepared for battle.

Dr. Allan Beall, MD
Interventional Cardiologist

INTRODUCTION

For a long period of time humanity has been fighting diseases, especially the ones that are directly connected to bad eating habits or the consumption of some foods or even alcohol, drugs, Tabaco, etc., which directly affect the human body. All of these harm our body's organs and, in the end, the lack of knowledge of these facts can cause death. It is usually called a "silent" disease till the diagnosis is pronounced, and in many cases, it is too late to treat with only medication. In other cases, the illness is inherited by the parents, who inherited it from their parents, and it's been in the family history for many generations, and many times there are no details about it. This is one of the reasons why doctors often ask about family history, to have an understanding of affects to take into consideration, and to have a bigger picture for what they could be facing – especially because at that point, it's not possible for them to change the patient's DNA that was already form with information from their ancestors.

We should try as many ways as possible to find out what our ancestors did or didn't do, with the purpose of knowing what we're fighting against, because many times we face adversity (diseases, vices, or any other hardship), what we're facing are things that we inherited; we should be prepared before that disrupted gene activates and begins to play havoc with our lives.

More than trying to do research or find out what we were supposed to receive materially from our ancestors; we should try to find out more about our ancestors' behavior and struggles. We also have to remember that our memory can also be influenced by our ancestors, and know that the only way to change this is through the blood of Jesus Christ. He is the only one who can change our nature, even our temperament that at some point in our lives we've bragged about, being inherited from our ancestors. We also need to keep in mind that the things we have today we will be transferring to our generations, this can be biological or spiritual, and this is the very reason why it is of utmost importance to be transformed, to achieve what God wants us to, in order to be more like Him, and He will finish what He has started in our lives.

Therefore if we are wanting to achieve transformation to evolve and achieve perfection, as it was mentioned before; humanly speaking, there are areas that we can focus on to accomplish it; however, there is one that belongs solely to God, and that perfection is the key to achieve perfection in other areas, and this is the perfection in our genetics, to be able to go back the way we were in our original state (when God created us).

We also need to know that, in the midst of the battle between light and darkness, while God creates, the enemy copies to advance his operation of error with deceit. He is known as the father of deceit. Before humanity fell, Lucifer saw how creation was multiplying, he looked for a way to disrupt genetics, and in that moment he did it through food. Of course, we understand that it was due to disobedience that Adam and Eve sinned and were casted away from the garden, but this was through food, it was a strategy that the enemy planned with the purpose of affecting all the generations that were to come, for them not to be perfect anymore. From this example we can understand that the battle between light and darkness also covers genetics, and the enemy has been fighting for thousands of years and our ancestors were partakers on this battle being victims and vessels to transfer this disruption.

For a long time, what was believed and accepted about genetic inheritance covered parents, grandparents, and great grandparents, 14 generations was the total of the genetic line that was taken into consideration. However, we must know that each one of us has a genetic line of 42 generations and each one of them another 42 that have influenced them to do what they did and left as a mark on their DNA and this was inherited to us, therefore we are now experiencing things from a genetic ghost, we don't know its origin and even though we might not know all the details this influence is part of our existence; unless we submit to the only way to transform our DNA, and this is through Jesus Christ blood; through communion we have access to that blood that can transform our DNA, and everything else that the enemy genetically disrupted will be cancelled and we can go back to our original state.

May this book be a guide and light to you, the reader. For you to understand what you can do to get rid of all those things that are disrupting your life, knowing that you can go to the only one who knows you and can regenerate you: our Lord Jesus Christ.

CHAPTER 1

THE EXPERT MINISTRY OF THE SOUL

Mario & Luz Rivera

One of the purposes of these teachings is for us to be able to understand why some conflicts arise from the soul, and to know how to solve them using tools that the Lord places for us, His people, His church, and to be used correctly, until we become experts in spiritual warfare. Obviously, in the bible you can find men who were experts in what they did, proving the quality of their job, and God allowed them to gain more experience through time to achieve the required professional-spiritual level.

A good example can be seen in the bible with the sons of the tribe of Issachar, who had understanding of the times knowing what Israel ought to do (1 Chronicles 12:32), this shows me that if God allows you to be an expert in something specific it is because you have a responsibility to share or impart it to others, even when you still have a lot to learn. The knowledge that He has allowed you to acquire is for others to know what to do in different situations in the spiritual realm.

As a minister of God you must know that you have a huge responsibility before Him since He's trusted you with the souls of people, therefore it is of utmost importance to know and understand how the soul works and how it was designed and what its job is as part of a whole.

The human being is tripartite that is spirit, a soul and a body. Therefore, the spirit has a function, the soul has a function and the body has a function as well but the soul is the most complex part because the soul operates between two dimensions; the celestial one in which the spirit operates and the physical one where the body operates. Therefore, it can be said that the soul is like a bridge and it is important for that bridge to be in good condition and to go through restoration processes when needed. This is also to understand that everything God sends through his Spirit to your spirit before getting to the body, goes through the soul as if going through a filter and when the body receives what was sent by God the body can use it (manage it, receive it) in a better way taking into consideration that it has an influence from the soul.

This is the reason that one of the most difficult things for a person to submit is their soul; in other words, the soul is the part of the tripartite being that mostly resists the work our Lord, Jesus Christ, is doing. In a way you could say that the soul is the area where the work God wants to do in a person is allowed. Remember, God is gentle, therefore the Holy Spirit won't force His will on you and He'll work in your life as much as you allow Him to. Even the enemy has no power to do anything in your life unless you allow him to, the problem is that if you open a door to him, he'll push it and try to destroy as much as possible. The greatest problem is therefore in the soul, even when doing ministry work by God's servants that bless the church; it is in the soul of the people of the congregation that the greatest conflict of opposition is found.

When God started the redemption work in your life, he started it in the Spirit; when you invited Jesus Christ into your heart and recognized Him as your Lord and savior your spirit was the first one to automatically receive that salvation. In fact, your spirit resurrected; since the bible says that the spirit was dead in sin but when Jesus entered your heart, He vivified your spirit.

The last thing to be rescued is the body, in a moment, in the twinkling of an eye, (1Cor 15:51-53), measuring it by time, in a millisecond; that's how the transformation of the body will happen and you'll have a glorious body no matter how your body is right now, or if you've been ill, if you're weak, etc., you'll be transformed. A problem that humanity is facing nowadays is that many people are focusing on accomplishing the results that only God can accomplish, humanity worships the body investing more time at a gym that connecting with God when God already established that He will perfect the body, but that'll be the last phase; first He'll perfect the human spirit when He vivifies it, the last phase will be to immortalize the human body, but, what will happen with the soul?

This is why now is a good time for you to seek restoration for your soul, to do all that is in your power for the Lord to continue His perfect work in you and this is where the importance of a ministry expert of the soul lays, because this is the area that causes the most conflict, even though sometimes you might think otherwise. Today you can learn how to help yourself with some things, and how to disconnect yourself from other things that might be influencing you to have a lifestyle that draws you apart from God's plan, not reaching the level you could have in your spirit and also in your soul. Because you can also be spiritual in your soul; remember, you cannot be spiritual in your human spirit but you can be celestial in your human spirit, however the soul can reach spirituality in the best case, or it can be from the flesh.

Many people tend to feel stuck in the evolution of becoming more spiritual because there might be something stopping them from reaching the level that they desire. **So, the question would be, what can we do to identify antagonistic situations in the soul of the people who need God's help?** I'll begin pointing out the following: the process of ministration of the soul is the tool that done by an expert that can help you remove what's hidden in the soul but also needs to follow some steps.

What is Ministration of the soul?

It is a process that the soul has to go through to show things that have been present just as symptoms (these can be situations or consequences that lead people to feel a certain way); these symptoms could be to be inclined to some things and not to be strong enough to reject them (even when knowing that these shouldn't be part of their life), like alcoholism, drug addiction, illicit sex, pornography, etc. Things that can cause harm in your body and that could be considered vices of the soul. Ministration can uncover all of these things through the Holy Spirit and these things can be treated being guided by Him. The cooperation of the person going through this process is also needed in order for his/her soul to be restored. In other words, it cannot be forced, the person going through this process has to want to be restored.

This will take you to the following steps:

- How to do a ministration of the soul?

- How to see all that is related to a ministration of the soul?

- How to start a ministration?

- How to apply the information gathered in a ministration to a deliverance?

Remember that ministration and deliverance are two different things, but one will lead to the other. Ministration helps people who might need counseling or to learn a disciplined way to live and redirect behaviors that are keeping him/her restless or even feeling guilty, but this is different to a deliverance of demons. Not all the people who go through a ministration process need deliverance, however in most cases deliverance is needed due to the lifestyle one has lived. Therefore, once a person has experienced a ministration it will lead them to the next step.

What are the Requirements of Someone in The Area of Deliverance?

The most important key for someone working in deliverance is to understand what can be done and what should not be done in a deliverance. Ignorance is a KEY FACTOR to defeat. The fight against the forces of darkness should not be done in ignorance, preparation is required for this task.

The Spiritual Realm: The spiritual realm is ruled by laws. The holistic preparation of the deliverer implies holiness and also training to acquire the knowledge of principalities that rule the battles:

1. Do not imitate spiritual warfare.

2. Do not confront the powers without understanding the ranks.

3. Do not get into battle for impartation alone and without understanding.

4. Do not try to go and cast away demons without first going before your authorities to be blessed, covered and to plan a strategy to use.

5. Do not get into battle if you have hidden (unconfessed) sin.

6. Do not get into battle if you don't have a devotional lifestyle.

7. Do not get into battle without having read bible verses about Jesus casting away demons.

8. Do not get into battle alone.

Because they're the experts on spiritual warfare...

A biblical scenario: contains the principles to take into consideration to know what to do and what not to do.

Acts 19 is the formula, it is very interesting to see how it portrays a scenario of the spiritual things that happen during a battle. It is like a battle manual.

(Acts 19:11-12) *[11]And God was doing extraordinary miracles by the hands of Paul, so that even handkerchiefs or aprons that had touched his skin were carried away to the sick, and their diseases left them and the evil spirits came out of them.*

The Groups that Imitate Spiritual Warfare:

Each time God manifests His POWER in spiritual warfare, there will be groups that are going to want to have the power without the preparation.

*(**Acts 19:13-16**)* ¹³ *Then some of the traveling Jewish exorcists also attempted to call the name of the Lord Jesus over those who had evil spirits, saying, "I implore you and solemnly command you by the Jesus whom Paul preaches!"* ¹⁴ *Seven sons of one [named] Sceva, a Jewish chief priest, were doing this.* ¹⁵ *But the evil spirit retorted, "I know and recognize and acknowledge Jesus, and I know about Paul, but as for you, who are you?"* ¹⁶ *Then the man, in whom was the evil spirit, leaped on them and subdued [a]all of them and overpowered them, so that they ran out of that house [in terror, stripped] naked and wounded.*

Do's and Don'ts:

#1 Do not imitate spiritual warfare:

- In spiritual warfare never try to IMITATE any other person, each person's identity is supported by God and respected by the spiritual realm.

- Falsification or imitation of identity WILL NOT be supported by God; this could be a way to give advantage to unclean spirits to attack the imitators, this is what happened to Scevas' seven sons when they tried to imitate Paul.

- Don't imitate anointing, don't imitate the shouts, or try to use formulas of invocations. Imitations in spiritual warfare is like breaking a wall to find a snake that will bite.

(Ecclesiastes 10:8 NCV)[8] Anyone who digs a pit might fall into it; anyone who knocks down a wall might be bitten by a snake...

The principles and the order are both important to observe in spiritual warfare. Imitation is punished because it is a demonstration of the POWER without the anointing. Whoever imitates will have to pay a price for that imitation.

#2 Do not confront the powers if you don't understand the ranks: Many people confront and even curses the fallen glories without understanding and knowing the principles of ranks (Jude 1:8-10)

#3 Do not get into battle just for impartation without the understanding: Don't cast away demons if you're not equipped or trained to do so; faith has to be part of the process but you also need training to cast away demons (Mark 16:17-19).

#4 Do not try to go and cast away demons without first going before your authorities to be blessed, covered, and to plan a strategy to use: It's not about lack of confidence or calling, it's about the ORDER in the spiritual realm (1Kings 22:19-22).

#5 Pray and Obey: Don't get into spiritual warfare if you have problems with OBEDIENCE. Prayer and disobedience do not create synergy of power, obedience is a principle that God has established as a key to victory. Many people make the mistake of trying to go to battle when they're in disobedience and the only thing they get is open doors to eventually be attacked and become a victim.

#6 Do not get into battle if you have hidden (unconfessed) sin: Don't try to go and cast away demons if there is bitterness, lack of forgiveness, jealousy, hate, rebellion, etc. If you try to cast out demons before submitting these areas (sin) to Christ, the unclean spirits will only go from the person who is being delivered to the person who is struggling with their unsubmitted areas. It is like giving space for *vector spirits* that are like fleas that jump from one place to the next, these can even be transferred to *the clothes* that the person doing the deliverance is wearing if these areas have not been submitted. Do not forget that the spiritual realm operates under "the regime of the rights" (Hebrews 12:15).

#7 Do not get into battle if you don't have a devotional lifestyle: To be successful as a person working in the area of deliverance, it is required for you to have a lifestyle that includes prayer and fasting. These two are key for us to be sensitive to the Holy Spirit's guidance. Remember, deliverances are not through "methods" but through God's guidance. It is necessary to have a life of devotion to God, where we have an "altar" to go to and present ourselves before God before going to battle (Matthew 17:14-21).

#8 Do not get into battle without having read bible verses about Jesus casting away demons: The secrets of spiritual warfare that Christ taught are there. When we read them, we fill up our spirits whit Christ's *rhema* that casts away demons. The more you read these verses the more you'll be filled with Christ's revelation (Matthew 4:4).

#9 Do not get into battle alone: There is a powerful reason behind the fact that at least two people are needed for spiritual warfare and it is God's strategy. Remember, **one** will defeat **a thousand** and **two ten thousand**. But it is also about protection and testimony of what happens (1Samuel 18:7).

Which Gifts Operate in a Deliverance?

Since ministration and deliverance cannot be guided by a manual of processes or solved as a logistics problem, the Holy Spirit is the only one that can guide you in what are the right steps to follow in order to liberate the soul of a person; but being guided by the Holy Spirit also requires principles and parameters in order to avoid manipulating someone's soul (even when that's unintentional). To avoid this from happening you will need the discernment that only the Holy Spirit can give you.

- HOW TO APPLY DISCERNMENT OF SPIRITS IN A DELIVERANCE? During a deliverance is where you'll need discernment of spirits, God will equip you with it, therefore you won't try things in vain but for you to be accurately focused in what you have to do to achieve victory.

Which are the spirits that attack men and women most frequently?

Spirit that most frequently attack women: <u>Spirit of disease</u>.

And behold, there was a woman who had had a disabling spirit for eighteen years. She was bent over and could not fully straighten herself. Luke 13:11 ESV

- Weakness
- Cancer
- Breast problems
- Diabetes
- Arthritis
- High blood pressure
- Bleeding
- Vaginal infections
- Strokes
- Fever
- Allergies

- Depression
- Hypertension

Spirit that most frequently attack men: <u>Spirit of slavery</u>.

For you did not receive the spirit of slavery to fall back into fear, but you have received the Spirit of adoption as sons, by whom we cry, "Abba! Father!" Romans 8:15 ESV

- Alcoholism
- Drug addiction
- Smoking
- Anorexia
- Bulimia
- Manipulation (from others)
- Codependence
- Sex addiction
- Workaholic
- Shopaholic

- TV addiction
- Porn addiction

How to End a Deliverance?

This is a very important step, the fifth one, because if you don't end it the right way, the demons could come back and the bible teaches us that they could come back with other seven worse than the one that left. Therefore, it is necessary to be covered by the blood of Jesus and rebuke any counterattack from the enemy. The fact of knowing how to end a deliverance will determine how much of an expert the man or woman that work with souls is.

One of the most awful things for a minister of God is not knowing anything about the soul, and dismiss the importance of it by not taking advantage of opportunities to work with it. Because the importance of it is not considered, you won't be able to work with your own soul or the souls of the members of your family and if you are in ministry you won't be able to work with the souls of the people of your congregation and they will not be able to experience spiritual growth and they will not be able to learn more about their souls. You could be asking right now: then, who knows the soul? And the only answer will be: Jesus, He is the expert in everything. Now, if we want to know if there are any men or women that know the soul, a good example would be David; he writes a lot about the soul, talking about situations in his soul, since he had lived many things as a consequence of problems in his soul.

How does a Deliverance Team Operate?

I have talked about this in other books, however I will try to go into more detail, the following bible verse will be the one I will use to do so:

¹ Brothers, if anyone is caught in any transgression, you who are spiritual should restore him in a spirit of gentleness. Keep watch on yourself, lest you too be tempted. ² Bear one another's burdens, and so fulfill the law of Christ. Galatians 6:1, 2 ESV

You won't see the word ministration itself, however the concept is coded in the bible; what I want to show to you here is that the people called to be restorers, have to have reached a spiritual level that has moved them from doing what their flesh asks them to, to have restored their own souls. One of the main problems that occur sometimes happens when the person who is ministering hasn't restored his/her soul, maybe because there hadn't been any problems —even though it is very difficult for someone to say that they've never had problems or that they've never struggled with their souls, even without knowing. The person ministering should have some experience before giving advice, of course in the end it is the Holy Spirit the one that talks through the person ministering, but even though we know that, it is not likely that he/she would give good advice without knowing what the other person is living in his/her soul, and that could harm the person that needs to be restored.

A good example of this is when a person has a problem and while looking to fix his/her problem, talks about it with a person today, another one tomorrow, and a different one the day after looking for advise. The problem gets worse when the person listening has had the very same problem but hasn't solved it, and because of it, his/her soul hasn't been restored and there is bitterness in his/her soul because the wound is still open. When this person hears about this problem, he/she is reminded of how this problem affected this person's life and that wound that hadn't healed properly reopens and starts bleeding and this makes this person give bad advice. Then the person in need of advice receives advice, but bad advice and this gets them into a vicious cycle, where this person will look for advice in the wrong place –not in a ministration process and will keep on getting bad advice and the problem will get worse every time because with each answer the person is not getting the restoration needed.

It is because of this very reason, that if at any given time you have a problem where ministration of the soul is vital, don't hesitate and ask for help. First of all because it is better for your soul and also because after being restored, you can reach a spiritual level that will allow you to restore others.

The Ministration Of the Soul

I'll will give as much detail as possible about this matter, trying to be as practical as possible to explain it in a way that is easy to understand, for you to have a clear idea of this very important matter:

- Probe the soul of the believer by the Spirit.

- Why do you probe? To know the past and present to receive help for the future.

To be able to probe; the person who is ministering needs participation from the person that needs help, otherwise the person ministering won't be able to break with whatever that needs to be broken. It is already enough to battle against the operation of darkness to also have to fight to find out what the matter is. It is necessary for the person who is being ministered to confess with their mouth any accusation that the enemy could use against this person about this person's past. All of this needs to happen this way since a spiritual law is operating there and it is the principle of confessing our sins to each other. Remember, the spiritual realm of darkness is a legal realm (world), that operates through rights; therefore, when someone doesn't confesses his/her sins, even when the person walked away from it, the spiritual realm has the right to influence that person.

Remember that first you have to confess and then you have to walk away from sin; the problem is that many times people want to change the process and don't even fulfill them because they pretend to walk away from sin without even confessing their sin, they don't look for help –ministration of the soul. Therefore, the kingdom of darkness still has legal rights over that person to intervene in the legal spiritual realm and it could be and internal or external intervention.

When I talk about a spiritual intervention, in the spiritual warfare connotation, we could talk about depression. It is called depression when it is internal, but we're not talking about the mental disorder, but a demonic operation operating inside a person. Different from oppression, because oppression is from the outside to the inside, it's when an obstacle appears in the environment of the person. Demons can determine a strategy, depending on the things you haven't confess, for example: a couple that is engaged, have done everything right and have a wedding date, but one of them asks the other to have sex since everything is already set for the wedding, they think it shouldn't be a problem and both agree to have sex.

In this example the problem is that they didn't know that this will create an appetite in their soul and if they don't confess their sin, that appetite will increase –but not to be just with their spouse, but to be with someone else and they will fall in adultery. Therefore ministration is one of the opportunities God gives to be able to confess any sin, whether you're single or married; but, if you don't confess your sin even if you walk away from it, the enemy will still have a spiritual legal right over this person and he won't hesitate on activating it anytime he pleases.

Another thing you should keep in mind is that restoration is a process, therefore and usually it doesn't happen immediately; salvation is immediate and you should take advantage of it when it is presented to you because it leads to other things:

1. Salvation of the human spirit

2. Eternal life

3. Name written in the book of life

And you can also see how Christ defeated the kingdom of sin and how the Holy Spirit through a divine process cleanses you from anything from your past.

What is not Ministration of the Soul?

It is not stimulation and psychological response. This is what is used in the movements called "Encounters," which is it's based in a Greek term:
CATHARSIS (Gr. Kathairein = Purify)

It's unloading emotions, where it is asked for them to cry, whether they want it or not and many times help is pretended to be given, making them remember unpleasant moments of their lives, moments where they were humiliated and their soul was harmed yet this is not ministration of the soul. I also need to mention that they set aside, better said they dismiss ministration and deliverance, in many cases because they don't believe that a Christian can have demons.

1. This isn't anything but a *purge* of the soul

    - In other words, freeing the mind from what acts as a hindrance.

    - This can happen when someone is "managing" other people's emotions, touching the emotions, making them imagine painful, hurtful or sad scenes. This person is manipulating the one in need through words, a letter, a sent message etc.

2. Reaching the emotional side of someone, will make that person have imaginary scenes.

- Imagining painful or moments of anguish, sadness or pride
- A person's emotions were manipulated through a word, letter or message received.

The ministration of the soul is completely different, it is biblical and it helps to discern the ministrations that were given to the soul at any stage of life:

1. From the womb
2. As a child
3. And throughout the different stages of growth

The ministration of the soul is going to probe your past, your present and will discern your future, without falling in the mistake of guessing. It is also important to keep in mind that you shouldn't ignore a message from God being sent to you through another channel. At times it may not be during ministration because God sends messages in many ways. This is another reason why you need discernment, to discern when a message is from God and when it is from your own soul. Remember: many of the problems in your present are linked to your past and threaten your future.

Ministration and The Present

If you identify a problem in your present, it is possible that you're breaking up with your past and your future will fulfil its destiny.

Ministration: Comes from the Greek word #1248 DIAKONEO, term that is found in this bible verse:

Are they not all ministering spirits sent out to serve for the sake of those who are to inherit salvation? Hebrews 1:14 ESV

The same Greek word is divided in three groups:

1. As a MINISTRY 16 times
2. As MINISTRATION 6 times
3. As MINISTERING 3 times

In general terms it means: to help, to serve, to meet the needs, to supply things necessary to live.

A Good Ministration Ensures a Good Deliverance

Ministration is the weapon that penetrates the spiritual dimension and transcends the ages. During the ministration the blood, flesh, holders (sin factory) and conjunctures are probed. The complete ministration to the soul is a deep work that is done by God's ministers with the help of the Holy Spirit to get rid of all contamination in the soul, however person being helped has to collaborate to reach the freedom that they desire. If the person leading the ministration asks odd questions, or at least odd to us, the person has to respond with transparency because if something stays hidden, then the enemy will take advantage of that moment to keep the sin hidden. If the person doesn't confess or respond sincerely. You need to keep in mind that when you are going through a process of ministration, the Holy Spirit will give you discernment to know where the problem is located, for example:

1. **The Blood:** It refers to the negative ancestors; they are like "the power (anti-anointing) from generational sin". **What's the importance of the blood during ministration?**

   For the soul of all flesh, its life, is in its blood. Leviticus 17:14 (Jubilee Bible 2000)

   The strength of the blood –negative strength- could come from the influence of negative ancestors.

   Our fight is not only with flesh and blood. Ephesians 6:12 (free translation)

   Pay close attention to the part that says *"not only"*... this term allows me to see that there is a literal fight, but it affects the spiritual realm.

   For you have not yet come <u>as far as to blood</u> in the struggle against sin. Hebrews 12:4 (ABIPE)

   This bible version allows us to see that there is also a battle in the blood but I want to highlight that the influence that is directly in the blood is a consequence of the ancestral inheritance that needs to be broken during the ministration of the soul.

God has been speaking to me in a very strong way about the ministration of the soul and the different processes, therefore it is needed to revisit what we already know with the purpose of not letting our guard down at any given time. If there is one thing, I have learned it is that whatever I have learned in this area of ministry at the beginning this same knowledge will be as real as the first time God revealed it to me. This is why I encourage you to review your knowledge about this and don't stop putting it into practice, in speaking about ministration. In order for it not to become a mere tradition that will lead to humanism and not something that the Holy Spirit has led you to do. Remember that these are end times and if your soul is deceived before leaving this earth, it is more likely that you'll need to return to cleanse your spiritual garments, to cleanse them in the blood of the lamb.

Based on the previously stated, I can see a parallelism with the Jewish feasts and ministration for example, in the **Passover** I see there is a calling for freedom, Jesus set you free through His sacrifice but you also need to keep in mind that the enemy is constantly attacking you to stain your garments. This is another reason to come to His table and participate in the Holy Supper (communion) and get a new beginning for your life and instead of having a deliverance you can have a decontamination. We all have to battle against contamination from our past deliverance overruled the works of the kingdom of sin but the contamination stayed and it needs to be cleansed the same as our minds need to be cleansed.

After that celebration, there is a **First Fruits Feast**, and it represents the fruitful life that God is calling us to live. You were set free and decontaminated and now you must bear fruit.

The **Pentecost** comes next and this represents the spiritual gifts from God.

The **Trumpets Feast** comes after and it represents the discernment to hear what God is speaking to the church through the primary ministers, however that discernment happens as part of the process that started in the Passover Feast.

The **Feast of Atonement** is about blood, which means that when we are born again in Christ, most of our negative ancestral inheritance have disappeared and the Lord's divine genetics has increased in your system. The following feast, the **Tabernacle Feast**, which symbolizes to inhabit. This shows that one is ready to be united with the Lord.

It is very interesting that, according to gynecologists, the 7 feasts match with the 7 most important stages of gestation of a baby; for example, the **Trumpets Feast** is the first day of the seventh month and the baby's ear is developed on the seventh month of gestation and from that point the baby is capable of recognizing the voices of his/her biological parents.

Another interesting fact happens during **Hanukkah, The Feast of Lights**, which is celebrated the tenth day of the ninth month and it matches with the time of delivery of the baby.

I make mention of all this because there is hope for your soul to be fully restored from all the negative inheritance from your ancestors. Whether you wanted it or not; you have an inheritance from the moment you were conceived but through Jesus you can go back to be the way God has originally designed you to be. The word restoration is related to getting something back to its original state and this is accomplished by Jesus' bloodshed.

The Bible, Science, and The Genetics

How did we get here?

Let's make a review of the history of genetic investigations:

In 1953 and article on the Helical Structure of DNA was published by two researchers, Francis Crick from the United Kingdom and James Watson from the United States, this became the cornerstone of the sequential processes. Later a sequencing of the human genome project proposal is presented in a scientific conference in 1984, in Utah. This project was approved by the United States Congress in 1988, the project formally launched in 1990 with a budget of three billion dollars.

The agenda was:

1. Determine the complete nucleotide sequence of human DNA and locate the genes.

2. Build physical and generic maps.

3. Analyze the genome from organisms used as research models.

4. Develop new technologies.

5. Analyze and debate the ethical and legal implications for individuals and society.

At that time, it was believed that the number of genes in humans was 100,000 genes.

In 1994 the first genetic map is published and in 1996 the physical map. In the year 2000 the first draft is available and on Monday June 26, 2000, the human genetic code was read for the very first time. This was the first draft of the human genome sequence and was from Hispanic, Caucasian, and Afro-American people (3 women and 2 men). Within that same investigation, new data on the genome were released that allowed us to see that it consisted of approximately only 30,000 genes, thus changing the orthodox idea that they had that it was 100,000 genes.

The final sequencing mapping of the human genome was published on April 14, 2003 under the name "Human Genome Project."

Genetic Heritage

1. According to studies, many of the diseases are inherited.

2. Other times genes are disrupted by unclean spirits or demons, in other words, spiritual influence from the darkness.

3. Sometimes because of a curse from God due to ancestral iniquity.

4. Later on, the parents inherit it to their children generation after generation.

This is a reason why during ministration blood and ancestors need to be taken into consideration.

Ancestors

The word ancestors is not on the bible, however because it is a term that refers to previous generations; it is in the bible when it comes to families.

Ancestor is:

The sum of what you are and what you've received from your ancestors.

According to the dictionary:

Inheritance is the group of physiological and anatomical characters that living beings inherit from their parents. So, it reflects a gift from your parents, even when is not something good and in the scripture that is called ancient ruins.

Who Are the Ancestors?

This word is relative to ancestors, of remote origin, referring to ancestors and parents (this is gene-ethics). You must understand that there are things that are inherited out of tradition and it could be good or bad teachings from your parents.

When we talk about ancestors and inheritance that we've received, we can analyze inheritance by looking at our parents, but when the soul is being ministered, you must know that you are the product of at least 14 generations that contributed in the genetic system of each person:

- 8 great-grandparents
- 4 grandparents
- 2 parents
- Me

According to this generational representation, you are number 15, from a generation divided in four stages. This leads us to believe that one could be fighting against something that comes all the way from one of your great-grandparents and this is now known as epigenetics. From there the term "EPI" that means: beyond. Because of this, there could be situations that you could be having without having a logic explanation, in your body and/or soul, as a consequence of what your ancestors did in the past. Your genetics were marked and when it multiplied that mark became part of the genetic; which can be manifesting now in the physical or spiritual realm. This is also a good way to explain how diseases like diabetes, eating disorders which come from our ancestors

It is interesting to see that after 9/11(the world trade center attacks) according to some genetics and psychology research, the children of women who were pregnant during this event were more likely to be born with PTSD, inherited from their mothers. These infants presented higher levels of stress; their souls needed to be healed. Epigenetics had an important role in this situation. If you want to see a biblical reference on this matter, observe the following:

Matthew 1:17-18 ASV [17] *So all the generations from Abraham unto David are **fourteen generations**; and from David unto the carrying away to Babylon **fourteen generations**; and from the carrying away to Babylon unto the Christ **fourteen generations**.* [18]*Now the birth*

of Jesus Christ was on this wise: When his mother Mary had been betrothed to Joseph, before they came together she was found with child of the Holy Spirit.

In other words, we are the product of 14 generations, we have 14 possibilities of having altered genetics within our DNA, not just when it comes to positive things but also the negative ones. Without knowing for sure what it was that our ancestors did and it will appear suddenly, therefore it is possible that we are still subject to any type of weakness inherited by our ancestors.

Generational Weaknesses

It remains from generation to generation because no one has fought against its consequences.

The sources:

1. Genetically inherited from the parents.
2. Learning from our parents' example.
3. Influenced by the genetic memory of the parents.

Reality:

1. Naturally: In Christ, this takes you to the next level.

2. Personality: it needs to change, your nature in Christ has changed but your personality didn't, therefore ministration is key to finally be a new creation. The good news is that this means that there is a chance to change. Before Christ you didn't have that chance but now you do. This means that anyone who belongs to Christ has become a new person. The old life is gone day by day. With each opportunity to be a partaker in the Lord's Table (communion), there is also an extraordinary opportunity to be made new if you have faith.

Influenced by our parents' genetic memory: Through epigenetics, sperm transfers genetic information to many generations.

Michael Skinner, is a biologist known worldwide and is famous for eliminating scientific dogmas. There was a belief that every human had 100,000 chromosomes and it was proven that not all of them were active. At one point these chromosomes were seen as trash however, this biologist proved that the human genome isn't a perfect theory and that humans are influenced by 30,000 chromosomes. But what happened with the 70,000 left? They simply don't exist. This research took him to focus in a branch of science that had not yet been discovered and he named it: Transgenerational epigenetics. This means that there is a gen-ethical memory, even of the experiences of the great-grandparents that some were known or visible and others in secret; But the ones that were kept secret and that they went to the grave with those secrets were not so hidden because they were written in the genetic memory, which means that the gene knows where it comes from and those experiences are recorded in the great-grandchildren.

A scientist has expressed that the life experiences of grandparents or even older ancestors, have caused genetic structural changes in eggs and sperm of their direct descendants, that is, children, grandchildren, great-grandchildren and this phenomenon is known as "transgenerational epigenetics".

You must also know that there are some switches that turn on and off, which can be explained as iniquity from another perspective. Iniquity is the vehicle of sin, it is where sin is conceived, it is the motivation to sin, this is why the bible tells us that the iniquity from the parents will visit their children from third and fourth generation. This statement might leave you wondering some things, especially since some bible versions don't say "visit" but "punish"; but when we investigate that word, we understand that God will visit more than one generation to allow us to work in reducing the generational effect inherited. And when God sees that you're working towards your restoration, He shows you mercy and delivers you from the things you need help with.

The ministration of the soul is to probe through the Spirit. The past, present and future it is what is being seen scientifically in relation to the ailments of the body, but they can only stay see that aspect, when in reality there is a spiritual world that directly affects your life. For this reason, in epigenetics it has been possible to verify the connection with the experiences of the parents in the past, affecting in the present and if it is not cut, it will bring strong consequences in the future for other generations that will come from the loins of the men towards the belly of the women.

Chapter 2

The Genetics Of Metamorphosis

Mario & Luz Rivera

For a while ago God has been disquieting my heart with the things that are key to refining the lives of people; It is something in which you are somehow informed by the different communication media. It is a good thing to have information, since it is through knowledge that you'll be able to be aware of what needs to chance to achieve perfection in your life. God will open your eyes to see (understand) what needs to change and then He will require you to do your part, since there are changes that only the mighty power of God can make, for example:

1 Corinthians 15:52 (NLT) ...in a moment, in the blink of an eye, when the last trumpet is blown. For when the trumpet sounds, those who have died will be raised to live forever. And we who are living will also be transformed.

Only God can transform a life in such a short time "the blink of an eye", which according to scientists, takes 11 milliseconds, no one else has the ability to transform lives like God does. However, the bible also talks about another type of transformation:

*Romans 12:2 (NLT) don't copy the behavior and customs of this world, but let God **transform** you into a new person by* *changing the way you think. Then you will learn to know God's will for you, which is good and pleasing and perfect.*

In the Greek, the term "transform" is represented by two different words, one refers to changing the way of thinking; which can be done by a person with God's help and the other refers to the type of transformation that needs to happen before we leave this earth in the rapture, meaning that it is the type of transformation that only God can do.

Based on this information, I realize that one of the things that we should learn as Christians is that we can be part of our transformation process, according to the bible our genetics need to be perfected. Therefore, we are no longer talking about a mere transformation but about perfection. Why do I say this? Because the bible says it clearly: *"This means that anyone who belongs to Christ has become a new person. The old life is gone; a new life has begun!"* (2 Corinthians 5:17 NLT), this shows that you have become a new person, this is not necessarily visible at this moment or in this dimension, but God under the prophetic and scatological perspective is taking you to a new era where you will achieve perfection even in your genetics.

Remember that each time God creates a new world, He creates it with creatures with perfect genes, based on this statement I can tell that the earth has gone through some recycling processes, if I may call it that way. The Bible allows us to see what happened before Genesis 1:1, it was a different era from the one mentioned; the first time Adam appears in the bible and the future era will be from the millennial kingdom onwards. There are therefore 3 eras, identified as the past, the present and the future. The link between one era and the next is <u>perfect genetic.</u> God begins the ages, with what he has allowed to reach perfection genetically speaking. This is why the Lord is preparing you in such a way, that you will not only be transformed but perfected, in order that you can also be genetically perfect to inaugurate the new era that will be eternal.

Maybe the first obstacle that you will find and struggle with will be <u>humanism</u>; because what people tell us is that nobody is perfect and this is even used as an excuse to deliberately sin. To see themselves fail and making mistakes could even be part of the delight of a person that is not willing to do anything to change his/her mindset, even less, allow God to make their lives perfect. However, the bible is clear when it says there are some areas in the life of the believer that can be perfected (not only transformed), so you can be perfect in a holistic way. This also allows me to see, in the bible, things that have to be perfected:

1. Perfect Love
2. Perfect Gift
3. Perfect Peace
4. Perfect Healing
5. Perfect Faith
6. Perfect Patience
7. Perfect Work
8. Perfect Freedom
9. Perfect Law (torah = Instruction)
10. Perfect Heart
11. Perfect Knowledge
12. Perfect Joy
13. Perfect Man
14. GENETICS

As you can see, the first thing that God wants for you to have is perfect love. When I say love, I'm talking about different types of love, this can be seen in the Greek culture. They have what it's known as *erotic* love, *filos* love, *estorge* love, and *agape* love; however, in the bible you will only find *filos love* which is the love among siblings, and *agape love* that is a perfect and spiritual love; this also teaches us that we should direct our love towards that direction, for our love to be perfect. The bible tells us:

1 John 4:18 *(ESV) There is no fear in love, but perfect love casts out fear. For fear has to do with punishment, and whoever fears has not been perfected in love.*

As I mentioned before, there are other things that can be perfected, but one cannot be substituted for another. However, if genetics are not perfected, the other thirteen mentioned will not be perfected either, if all thirteen were perfected and the genetics have not been perfected, one will continue battling with that ancestral heritage, which may even go back as far as great grandparents. In other words, if you are not perfected in love, you will believe that you love a person, but when some inconvenience arises, hatred can be greater than anything. Likewise, with peace, you can have it but it will be very easy to lose it if your genetics is not perfected and you can come to live in a total contradiction of your personality, even having double personality, which is known as a bipolar person.

People who are struggling with this kind of battle are suffering from what is also known as a paradox, because that person has good and bad things at the same time, part of his or her life is full of light and the other part full of darkness. At some point that same person could be ministering the word of God and people are being blessed but at the end it could be that that person returns to his previous state due to ancestral inheritance that weighs on him/her or perhaps their receptor of vices is manifested. Which does not allow there to be total perfection, which can leave you out of the group to which God is calling you, because what He wants is to start a new time, with people who have managed to understand the need that genetics cannot remain on the side of their life, but they have come to understand that **regeneration** is necessary.

You will also notice that this is a compound word, the first one is a prefix that indicates that the other word will have a new incidence, its application regarding genetics, means that the genes will go back to their original state. This allows us to see the process of that wonderful gift, that the Lord Jesus Christ gave us through his sacrifice on the cross, where the element of salvation and redemption was the blood of Christ, the blood of the Lamb of God, perfect and divine blood that guarantees if you allow it to substitute the

genetics that you inherit- the opportunity of DNA's regeneration.

Regeneration

The etymology of regeneration:

1. Regeneration: Go back to the original genetics, to recover yourself...

2. Re = prefix that suggests going back to the origins...

3. Gen = genetics...

4. Eration = descendants with the same genes, and/or a same time or age...

If the prefix RE is taken away from the word REGENERATION it wouldn't exist if you don't apply an etymological interpretation, I mean, the proper origin, way, usage, and composition of the word. In other words, there cannot be GENERATION or GENETICS without the GENE or GENES, therefore when the bible talks about REGENERATION it talks about

God wanting our genetics to be transformed to the original state, the way He created it to be, in a way that everything that has been affected by ancestral heritage will be eliminated to a point that there won't be temptation that will make you fall, and there won't be any inclination to sin because everything has been completely restored.

Therefore, when we talk about ancestors, we talk about genetics; and when we talk about genetics, we cannot leave aside the new age of genetics, the **epigenetics**. This is something that wasn't made up by us, it is something that scientists discovered, and we know that the term EPI in Greek means "go further or beyond", with this you can understand that epigenetics means: beyond genetics; genetics beyond the conventional or orthodox. This is a very good reason to take this seriously, because if you don't pay attention to the meaning and power of Christ's sacrifice, it would have been in vain.

The blood of Christi s not only useful for spiritual warfare, it has a power that goes beyond that and you are directly involved so you can achieve the divine nature that the bible talks about:

2 Peter 1:4 *(ESV) by which he has granted to us his precious and very great promises, so that through them you may become partakers of the divine nature, having escaped from the corruption that is in the world because of sinful desire.*

Why is this important?

1.   The word re-generation is founded the word generation.

2.   The word generation comes from the word GEN or GENES.

3.   GENES is related with gene transfer.

4.   Genetic transference means transfer genetics information to the next generation.

5.   It is also a message to the next generation: you will be the same as the previous generation.

You have to also consider that if the DNA was disrupted in the physical and in the spiritual, it will still transfer all the information; the vessel that receives it will be the bridge for the next generation plus whatever the vessel adds and so on.

When you analyze who you are, you have to understand that you are the sum of all of your ancestors. In other words, you have the makeup you didn't ask for, however, it was in you to be activated automatically whether you wanted it or not. Put it in different words, these are like the default apps that come in mobile device, you didn't ask for them, however, they are there and they could be activated at any given time. The ancestral heritage is there and it sometimes manifests as mood swings, behavior changes and reactions that you don't understand or recognize in yourself, these things are just waiting to be activated.

The Genetic Battle

All of this is very interesting because there is a genetic battle that is marked throughout the bible and history. You should consider that the kingdom of darkness also knows what it can achieve when a generation, family, or individual is attacked in their genetics and this is why through the bible God allows you to see how historically genetics were the weapon the enemy used to affect humanity.

> 1. In the beginning the spiritual genetics was contaminated:

Romans 5:12 *(ESV) Therefore, just as sin came into the world through one man, and* *death through sin, and so death spread to all men because all sinned—*

The bible teaches us that it was through sin that death genetic appeared, even without being born, all of us can be considered sinners and worthy of death, because sin affected the genetics of the father of creatures that were meant to be like him.

2. The mixture of human genetics continued:

Genesis 6:4 *(KJV) There were giants in the earth in those days; and also after that, when the sons of God came in unto the daughters of men, and they bear children to them, the same became mighty men which were of old, men of renown.*

What happened here is that divine beings got together sexually with mortal women and from those relationships a hybrid race emerges.

3. Genetic manipulation is possible nowadays.

Jude 1:19 *(ESV) It is these who cause divisions, worldly people, devoid of the Spirit.*

The advances in science have come to a point of human cloning, these humans don't have a spirit nor a soul, because only God can give these. Mankind has discovered, through the human genome, how to make humans. This research has also allowed them to open a cell and find all the genetic information so a human can be created according to their taste and desires, when they collect the embryo, they can manipulate it and then artificially fertilize it. The question that pops up at this stage is: does this new being have a human spirit? Since the human spirits come from God and you cannot live on this earth without a spirit, if you are not filled by God you'll be filled by the enemy.

Therefore, where there is genetic manipulation and the process that God established is not there, meaning the divine law for human creation, God doesn't give His breath of life so that embryo manipulation doesn't get a human spirit. However, since the unclean spirits are human without redemption, then the enemy places an unclean spirit in that being.

4. Genetic restoration or Regeneration:

***Matthew 19:28** (BLB) And Jesus said to them, "Truly I say to you that in the regeneration, when the Son of Man shall sit down upon His throne of glory, you* *having followed Me, you also will sit on twelve thrones, judging the twelve tribes of Israel.*

Titus 3:5 *(BSB) He saved us, not by the righteous deeds we had done, but according to His mercy, through the washing of new birth and renewal by the Holy Spirit.*

This is why in the latter days, the world will be inhabited by people with human spirits, with the spirit of Christ, with the Holy Spirit, and the Father's spirit; that's the group of people you belong to, but you also need to know that there are humans with unclean spirit, due to genetic manipulation as part of the operation of the kingdom of darkness against regeneration of those who have been called by Christ, which sole purpose is to get them stuck in the regeneration process.

What God is doing today is regenerating those men and women that have Christ in their hearts, and this is hope for you, and this is why it is so important for you to understand the need of genetics transformation for you.

Orthodox Guide of Ancestors

Everything you've read up to this point, is also very connected with what you know about ancestry and this takes us to the idea of a family tree. Why a tree? Remember that a tree has 4 parts:

1. Root.
2. Trunk.
3. Branches
4. Fruit.

And these represent the following:

1. Great grandparents
2. Grandparents
3. Parents
4. Myself

Even though this is a genetic orthodox guide, it is necessary to widen the picture for you to see all the way through this family tree.

The "I" part is represented by you, in other words, you are the result of the sum of 14 people, that is the orthodox and is called ancestor of the genetic or simply genetics. However, God has left an encrypted message in the bible to make you realize that you are the sum of more than 14 people. Just by realizing that you have or had 8 great grandparents, that you might or might not have met can be a little unsettling especially when you analyze or think about the things they might or might not have done; you simply don't know and when we talk about genetics it is even harder to know. The years involved seem just such a short period of time when you put them next to the epigenetics point of view, for example:

Traditional genetics: We've talked about genetics in 3rd and 4th generation:

1. Great grandparents

2. Grandparents

3. Parents

4. Children

Total: 14 people involved that give a total of 15.

Based on the lifespan found in Psalm 90, we would have a genetic history that would look like this:

Psalm 90:10 *The years of our life are seventy, or even by reason of strength eighty; yet their span is but toil and trouble; they are soon gone, and we fly away.*

1. We're talking about 840 years (when we multiply 14*60 years = 840 years)

2. Another calculation is when we take use the bible's example from Psalm 90:10, about 70 years of a life, 14*70 = 980 years...

3. The ones with more strength live 80 years, 80*14 = 1,120 years.

But when I talk about epigenetics, it means that even the Bible talks about the fact that you are the sum of more than 14 people, pay attention to the following:

Beyond Genetics: The Ancestors

Matthew 1:1 *(ESV) The book of the genealogy of Jesus Christ, the son of David, the son of Abraham.*
Matthew 1:17 *(ESV) So all the generations from Abraham to David were fourteen generations, and from David to the deportation to Babylon fourteen*

generations, and from the deportation to Babylon to the Christ fourteen generations.

With these verses I can see that we are not only the sum of 14 (ancestrally speaking), but the sum of 3 times 14, or said in a more direct way, you are the result of the sum of 42 people and so on. Each person that is part of those 42 has 42 ancestors; specialists in genetics say that the ancestral data can be deleted in 2600 years, but nowadays it is impossible to live that long, so there has to be something that accelerates the genetics transformation, in time and space.

It is because of this information that it is so important for us to understand the biblical ways for us to have a genetic transformation. This process may take a while and it will depend on the importance that you give to what God wants to do with you. Because you are the right person, the chosen one to change your family history, so your generations will be different, with different genetics than your ancestors, without the struggles and battles you had to face without information about why were you facing them.

I will show you a list of names that the studies have assigned according to ancient ancestry:

1. Father

2. Grandfather

3. Great Grandfather (Second grandfather)

4. Great- great- grandfather (Third grandfather)

5. 3X Great- Grandfather

6. 4X Great - Grandfather

7. 5X Great - Grandfather

8. 6X Great - Grandfather

9. 7X Great - Grandfather

10. 8X Great - Grandfather

11. 9X Great - Grandfather

Each one of these members of the family tree, is connected with 42 people that came before them, so if you want to know where you come from and what are the things God wants to regenerate in you, you will be able to see it in the following chart:

Los Ancestros

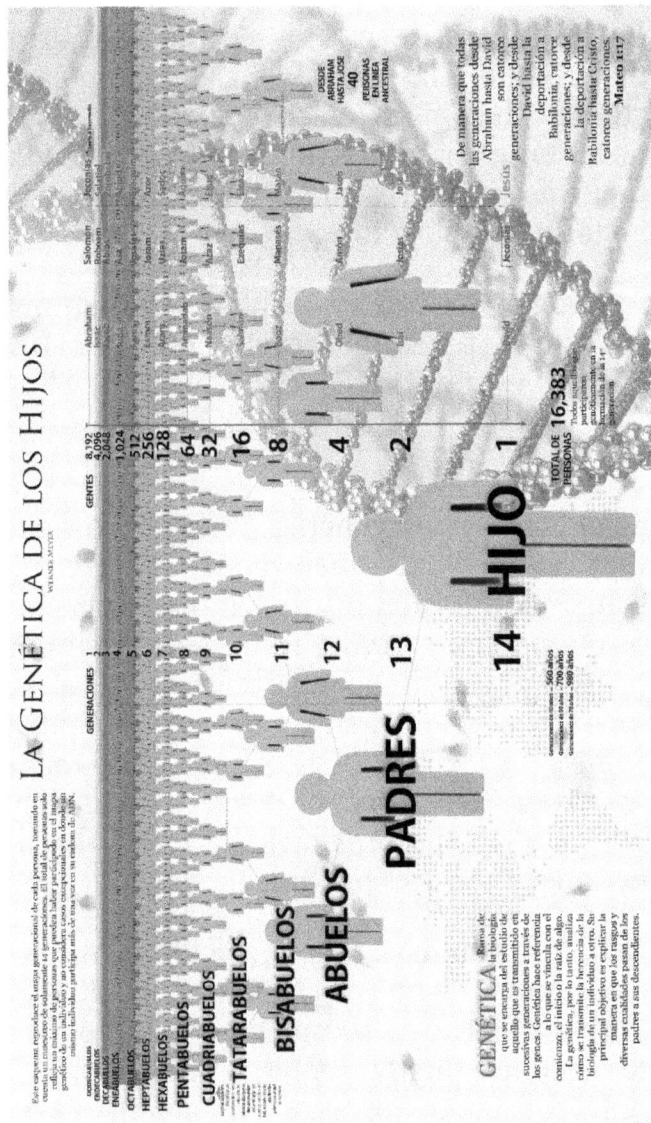

Image provided by the pastor of Ebenezer Ministries NY, Werner Meyer.
Http://ebenezerny.us

It is very interesting to see the quantities here, they match the measurements of storage that many electronic storage units have; another interesting thing to notice is that this chart presented each ancestor with a life span of just 30 years.

Although I have previously mentioned this, you must remember that EPIGENETICS means <u>beyond</u> GENETICS.

Epi = Beyond

Scientifically: epigenetics refers to a gene that is off, but when it is activated it transfers information that impacts the life of the person carrying it, because each one of us has an unimaginable ability to store memories, even when we cannot remember something. So, the story of our lives is made up from the story of each person that appeared in the previous chart and that is no longer genetics but epigenetics.

Now that you have this information you can ask yourself: who am I? What is inside me? Why do I struggle so much? When it comes to genetics, many people want to inherit only the good, physical characteristics or good qualities, problem being that in epigenetics you can inherit experiences, like difficult times that your ancestors went through, toxic environments, spiritual contaminations, if one of them did something in secret and nobody found out, this struggle might manifest in your life and you wouldn't know why.

It is because of this, that in order to change your epigenetics, it is necessary to go to the root of your ancestors, even when you don't know their names. However, by faith and the power of the word of God you can break with all of it and be transformed into a new breed. You will be able to experience this with your children, they'll have qualities, virtues from God, gifts from the Spirit that you don't have, they will have an intellectual capacity that you never imagined since you didn't see it in yourself. You thought all these things were impossible to achieve but when all the ancestral curses are broken there is an opportunity for a new beginning in your family history. From heaven you will be seen as a patriarch or matriarch you will be recognized as the person that stood on the road and asked about the eternal path, marked by God to walk on it in holiness.

Defending Epigenetics

Epigenetics is the study of the changes in genetic expressions that occur as a result of life conditions. It also allows us to see the way these changes could affect next generations.

People who have dedicated their time to study this, specifically genetic alterations, say that the descendants from the holocaust survivors had high levels of stress. First of all, they got to hear about their parents or grandparent's experiences for a long period of time, but then they realized that other generations which had not heard about these experiences directly from the survivors had the same levels of stress. Then there were 2 groups, one that heard the experiences first hand and the other that didn't. This made them understand that stress can be inherited.

This leads me to believe that there are many problems in Christian people that are considered psychological, however it could be the result of events lived by their ancestors, that caused this trauma and today they could be struggling with something as a result of a trauma experienced by an ancestor. I could also mention physical diseases that are inherited like diabetes, but also the famine that a previous generation lived could also manifest. In fact, world powers brand Central American people as a third world country or countries that have been colonized. Central America has been batteling with constant poverty. They have been affected by a toxic environment while working in the fields and pesticides have affected their respiratory system, to the point that many have died, however they have had children, and that allows epigenetics to present a combination of diseases that people have never seen before and suddenly they appear and it cannot be explained since you're looking for explanations in your parents and grandparents but this goes farther than that.

Another difficult situation to face is sexual abuse, this could happen because there were ancestors who went through this situation, it is something that needs to be seen as something that isn't random because there was a receptor in the blood, it wasn't active but that doesn't mean it wasn't there. The important thing about this is that these things have to be discussed in order for next generations not go through the same thing in order for no transmitting spirit to cast an attack against your offspring; God wants your offspring to be perfect to avoid situations like this one.

Epigenetics establishes that your genes could change according to your life style:

1. If you decide to live in a different way than your ancestors and according God's will, that could affect your generations and alter the genetic information you had from your ancestors and this is why you should decide to live a different life.

2. If even while knowing God you decide to live your life like your parents did, that could affect the life of your offspring even when they don't live their lives as you did.

Noah's Perfect Genes

Noah lived a life without genetic contamination, set aside from the mixtures that was present and the behavior from men in that time.

Genesis 6:9-10 *(NASB) 9These are the records of the generations of Noah. Noah was a righteous man, blameless in his time; Noah walked with God. 10Noah became the father of three sons: Shem, Ham, and Japheth.*

You can see that Noah had not been contaminated like everyone else, and if you add to this the lineage from which he came, you realize the type of genes he could have had.

Parallel to Shem is Cain, however his descendants experienced the flood, while Noah was delivered from this. The problem is in the responsibility of each generation for what they will do, for their life style and also if someone activates something that was previously deactivated. For example: base on the fact that ancestral heritage can be broken, I can say that there are many ways of doing that; some to accelerate time, like deliverance, however there are people that don't get the chance to be delivered, but they can find other ways to change their genetics. Sometime we participate in opportunities to be delivered (released) and due to lack of knowledge, those opportunities are not appreciated as they should be. Sometimes we identify things that allow us to advance in our genetics metamorphosis and we are more aware of receiving God's word and to take advantage of what we're receiving.

Biblical Example Of Epigenetics

Ham's life style:

Ham picked a wicked lifestyle that affected his descendants, that's epigenetics.

Genesis 9:22-23 *(NASB)* ²² *Ham, the father of Canaan, saw the nakedness of his father, and told his two brothers outside. ²³But Shem and Japheth took a garment and laid it upon both their shoulders and walked backward and covered the nakedness of their father; and their faces were turned away, so that they did not see their father's nakedness.*

Canaan's cursed epigenetics:

Genesis 9:24-25 *(NASB) ²⁴When Noah awoke from his wine, he knew what his youngest son had done to him.²⁵So he said, "Cursed be Canaan; A servant of servants he shall be to his brothers."*

Noah had knowledge of what we know nowadays as epigenetics. He knew his genes were perfect, therefore when he cursed Ham, epigenetically speaking, he cursed Ham's generations. This is why you should be careful with everything you do, because there is always a consequence (a good one or a bad one).

Ham's decision, epigenetically speaking, resulted in a curse to one of his descendants, that later became a group of people who lived in a land disowned by God and were conquered afterwards and considered God's enemies. All of this because a bad decision from one of their ancestors.

Epigenetics establish therefore that genes can be changed by a lifestyle. If you decide to live a bad life, doing what is not right before God, that will change the structure of your ovules (women) or sperm (men) and will transfer this experiences when you conceive and this will be imprinted or imported to your generations and usually the great grandsons/daughters are the ones who experience their ancestors' experiences.

All that you've read so far, is the result of studies that God has allowed me to develop, it is not something made up by me, is the sum of information with the purpose of understanding the powerful work that Jesus can do in your life through his blood, regenerating you. You have to ask the Holy Spirit to reveal to you those negative things that you've inherited, keep the good things but cast away the bad ones.

Your grandparents' experiences, or the experiences lived by ancestors before them, have made structural changes to your genes changing your ovules or sperm, it will affect your children, grandchildren, and great-grandchildren. This is known as Trans generational genetics. Genes keep track of where they come from, and humanly speaking it is impossible to change this information from your genes, only through a divine intervention by the power of our Lord Jesus Christ this can be done.

You are blessed because God chose you to change any Trans-generational alteration you may have.

The Science Of The Epigenetics

The formation of ovules and sperm:

The environmental information is imprinted in the ovule and the sperm since they are formed. Science has discovered that the environment can be captured by the ovules and sperms and the memories of experiences can be transferred and can affect the grandchildren of future generations.

The guardians of the genome:

I believe each person needs to be a guardian to its own genome, taking into consideration that each situation you go through will not only affect you but your descendants. You cannot just say: it's my life, I'll do this or that.

Deuteronomy 6:1-2 *(NASB) ¹"Now this is the commandment, the statutes and the judgments which the LORD your God has commanded me to teach you, that you might do them in the land where you are going over to possess it, ² so that you and your son and your grandson might fear the LORD your God, to keep all His statutes and His commandments which I command you, all the days of your life, and that your days may be prolonged.*

This is amazing that it is precisely in the end times when the Lord Jesus Christ is about return, that He is allowing us to see all of these situations with the purpose of achieving perfection in our lives. Weather this seems to be possible or not. You also have to have the desire to achieve it, you are part of the last generation of Christians and that consequently you will enter the new Earth with totally perfect genetics.

Chapter 3

The Internal Genetic Battle

When we speak about metamorphosis, we talk about a change in something specific, in this example I'm talking about genetics in regarding to the de-generation suffered for generations. Scientifically speaking, as I mentioned before, it is impossible for a person to be restored because of all the disruption suffered (genetically speaking) for generations, I even mentioned that, according to experts in genetics 2,600 years are needed to delete all the genetic information of things that have impacted a person; however today you have the hope that change is possible if you trust our Lord Jesus Christ. From here I'll begin with the Bible verse that will be the base to develop this chapter:

***2 Corinthians 5:17** (NLT) This means that anyone that belongs to Christ has become a new person. The old life is gone, a new life has begun!*

There are two processes, the old one stopped because the new one that comes from Christ disabled it as soon as you asked Jesus Christ into your heart. This is stablished through faith. However, you can also see it from a personal point of view, where responsibility is required to be able to supervise ourselves, to make sure the old life is gone and to know that the new life came to replace those things we received as inheritance; those ancestral influences we received, good and bad have been completely canceled but we need to be aware of what those are to battle against them.

We also see that this Bible verse talks about a new life and this new life is to live in a new world and it will be inhabited by believers like you. We are part of this new breed but in order for that change to have taken place, there needed to be a transformation in the genetic of every person. However, while you are on the way to perfection, you will suddenly find yourself in situations that are typical of disrupted genetics. You are certainly a new creature because that is what the Bible says, **but could it be that your old way of living has already been erased?** Although the Bible clearly lets us see that this will be the last part to be transformed with the sound of the final trumpet, in that moment there will be a transformation taking place in the blink of an eye. This is why it is necessary to learn things that by faith are considered completed even though we are not literally seeing them.

When you say you have eternal life, you can say it by faith, but you are not in eternity yet. This is as if you had a ticket to fly but you haven't used it yet so you're not there yet but you know when you're getting there; but in reality, to leave a life of sin and begin a new life is a matter of processes. For this reason, it is needed to understand the purposes of things you experience on daily basis, because if you don't, it will be hard for you to enter the promised land that the bible mentions. It is therefore necessary to be genetically perfect, since that is one of the ways God works when there's a new land. Noah is a good example of this:

Genesis 6:9 *(NLT) This is the account of Noah and his generations. Noah was a righteous man, the only blameless person living on earth at the time, and he walked in close fellowship with God.*

Now, when you do some research on the word *generations* its origin is in the word *genetics*, the one comes from the word *genes*. Therefore, it is necessary for you to see the origin of the word with the purpose of understanding God's vision in what He wrote for us. From this verse I can understand that Noah had perfect genes and this was the reason why God chose him and his family, to have the opportunity to re-start earth. God works this way, He chooses what has been regenerated, what is already perfect for a new beginning. The question then would be: Do we have perfect genetics? Remember, God doesn't do things without a reason or a purpose. If God is saying that He'll transform you (genetically speaking), it is because your genetics have been disrupted and He wants to regenerate your DNA, considering that you inherited your ancestor's way of living, we understand that you could have inherited good things, but sadly, most of the things we inherited are not good. God's desire is that we are perfected. There is a humanist thought that tells us that nobody is perfect, however, you can stop that though and pursue the perfection that God is achieving in your life.

What is Perfection?

It is commonly known as the condition of something that is perfect. Something perfect is something without a flaw, or defect. Something that has reached the highest level.

Many people say that they are not perfect; that they have flaws and others around them must simply deal with this because nobody is perfect. However, you can see in the bible that there are things that need to be perfected, this thought of nobody being perfect loses its value. When we study this, we find words in the Strong's dictionary, that talk about perfection:

1. Tamiym H8549
2. Shalem H8003
3. Tam H8535
4. Tummiym H8550
5. Miklah H4357
6. Kaliyl H3632
7. Teleios G5046

Six words from the Old Testament and 1 from the New Testament, and they all talk about perfection. From here we get a list of things that are perfect and even though I wrote this before, I will list these things again:

1. Perfect Love
2. Perfect Gift
3. Perfect Peace
4. Perfect Holiness
5. Perfect Peace
6. Perfect Patience
7. Perfect Work

8. Perfect Freedom

9. Perfect Law (The Torah = Instruction)

10. Perfect Heart

11. Perfect Knowledge

12. Perfect Joy

13. Perfect Man

14. **GENETICS**

I also mentioned before that none of these can substitute the other, however, you can see that number 14 is genetics and I wrote it this way to let you decide the level of priority this will have in your life. Said in another way, if you reach perfection in 13 things, but you don't reach perfection regarding your genetics, it is like the root of a contaminated tree hasn't been curated, even if the fruit and leaves had been curated, after a while, it will give bad fruit again; therefore, your priority should be to reach perfection regarding your genetics, therefore you will automatically achieve all the other perfections. Remember that to be part of the wedding feast of the Lamb, you must be perfect, so you need to work to make your genetics perfect, even though your genetics have been disrupted, God will restore you and make your genes perfect.

Therefore, to clean the earth, the flood was necessary, to restart the earth with a man with perfect GENES; in other words, to restore imperfect or contaminated GENETICS, God uses perfect genes. Sadly, the earth is corrupted again and one of the things corrupted is GENETICS and it needs to be restored for us to be genetically PERFECT.

How is this restauration going to take place? Through Jesus Christ's blood, through faith, through self-supervision, which will allow us to see that some ancestral manifestations will cease and instead you will see the divine influence form our Lord Jesus Christ. This is how you must continue living, participating from the Lord's supper at any given opportunity, as part of the preparation to be ready for His second coming when He comes for His church, His bride.

The Genealogical Line

I believe it is important to mention this again, and it's the orthodox idea of ancestors, or classic genetics. What we learned is that you are the result of 14 ancestral genetics, therefore you are number 15 in the family tree and this is known as direct blood link. Also, there is a collateral blood link, that is something genetics scientist know and to give you a clearer idea of what I'm talking about:

1. Direct blood link: Vertical

2. Collateral blood link: Horizontal

The Blood Bond

The consanguinity, from the biological point of view, implies that two people share a family tree, therefore they have the same ancestors. It is what is understood as a *blood bond* and it has various grades: the closer you are in the family tree, the closer the grade is.

The father-son relationship has the highest grade of bond (grade 1) since the genetics of children comes 50% from the father and 50% from the mother. Among grandparents and grandchildren, the grade is lower, only 25%, between uncles and nephews it is 12.5% and so on.

The bible talks about more than 14 people when it talks about ancestors, and it talks of three times fourteen = 42 people connected with another 42 and so on. In the end, it is an average of 1764 people.

The verses I'm about to share, have been mentioned before, but I believe it is important for you to keep them in mind regarding ancestry:

Matthew 1:1 *(NLT) This is the record of the ancestors of Jesus the Messiah, a descendant of David and of Abraham.*

Matthew 1:17 *(NLT) All those listed above include fourteen generations from Abraham to David, fourteen from David to the Babylonian exile, and fourteen from the Babylonian exile to the Messiah.*

Here I can see that, as a man but without sin, Jesus has an ancestral structure. Observe the first group of 14:

1. Abraham to Isaac
2. Isaac to Jacob
3. Jacob to Judah (TAMAR)
4. Judah to Perez
5. Perez to Hezrom
6. Hezrom to Ram

7. Ram to Amminadab
8. Amminadab to Nahshon
9. Nahshon to Salmon
10. Salmon to Boaz (RAHAB)
11. Boaz to Obed (RUTH)
12. Obed to Jesse
13. Jesse to king David

Between Matthew 1:1 and 1:17 one can clearly see Jesus' genealogy. Now pay attention to the next group:

1. David to Solomon (BATHSHEBA)
2. Salomon to Rehoboam
3. Rehoboam to Abijah
4. Abijah to Asa
5. Asa to Jehoshaphat
6. Jehoshaphat to Jehoram
7. Jehoram to Uzziah
8. Uzziah to Jotham
9. Jotham to Ahaz

Los Ancestros

10. Ahaz to Hezekiah
11. Hezekiah to Manasseh
12. Manasseh to Amon
13. Amon to Josiah
14. Josiah to Jehoiachin

I didn't add David to this group since he's already part of the first group. Now we have 28 people, we are still missing a 14 people group:

1. Jehoianchin to Shealtiel
2. Shealtiel to Zerubbabel
3. Zerubbabel to Abiud
4. Abiud of Eliakim
5. Eliakim to Azor
6. Azor to Zadok
7. Zadok to Akim
8. Akim to Eliud
9. Eliud to Eleazar
10. Eleazar to Matthan

11. Matthan to Jacob

12. Jacob to Joseph, the husband of Mary

13. Jesus, who is the Messiah

Among the many things that I can see to explain here, there is the fact that it does not say that Joseph begets Jesus, but only appears as the husband of Mary; because Jesus was begotten in Mary by the Holy Spirit; that's where all genetic inheritance is disconnected from Jesus. This is why the Lord has no connection with that ancestral inheritance. He is the initiator of a new Earth together with those who change genetics through Him and who will participate in the inauguration of that Earth that the Bible mentions, after all things have passed. But the point is that Jesus was disconnected from all that inheritance so that His genes would be kept pure and without any blemish, so that from Him you have the opportunity for perfect genes. I will also teach you how genetics degenerates and restores, as well as what things can transform genetics; however, there is something interesting that I want to show you:

There is a bible verse that shows us the importance of revelation about the GHOSTS in our GENES (INIQUITY) and understand where some of the struggles come from. Another bible verse REVELES the GHOST that is hidden in the blood:

Hebrews 12:4 *(AMP) You have not yet struggled to the point of shedding blood in your striving against sim.*

Hebrews 12:4 *(ASV) Ye have not yet resisted unto blood, striving against sin.*

This is nothing else but shedding your iniquity.

The Golgi Apparatus

In our bodies there is a Golgi apparatus and this is found in the cells and has a vital role in the transmission of genetics from our ancestors.

Its name comes from the scientist that discovered it functions in 1898 whose name was Camilo Golgi.

The Golgi apparatus is also called complex or Golgi body and it is responsible for the distribution and delivery of chemical products to the cell. The notion of apparatus can refer to the grouping of elements, that acting in a coordinated way and together, develop the same function. There are multiple apparatuses: among them, the Golgi apparatus. The Golgi apparatus is the organelle found in eukaryotic cells that is in charge of completing the production process of certain proteins.

It is also responsible of directing the molecular traffic of information and life experiences in protein form of the cell. Once the information is transformed into protein, it is transferred to DNA to feed them, but it really is a deception because if they are bad experiences, that protein is only a disguise so that your DNA does not reject it and is your daily food; but the blood of Christ in you will never receive your ancestral experiences to turn them into proteins because His blood already brings its own divine protein, so it is impossible for Golgi to transfer information to it.

The Golgi apparatus is found next to the nucleus in a cell, the nucleus is the one that keeps the DNA. It is an important part of the cell that **collects and stores generational behaviors, the stories and the memories, that will be transferred to the following generations**. Inside every cell of every human being there is a Golgi apparatus. The Golgi complex is a form of several groups of cisterns that are covered by membranes and have a disk shape. Each cistern forms a   structure like the plates from a battery. The Golgi complex has many vesicles that are used to send molecules to the cellular membrane where they are excrete. There are also bigger vesicles, that are used for selective excretions.

Iniquity is the sin of great grandparents, that find their way to us through the storage in the Golgi apparatus.

All of this means that among your genes there are years of information, therefore if you are in   Christ, you are made new, the old life is gone, the experiences from your ancestors are gone, and you'll have a new life.

The Golgi Complex

At some point, almost all the information molecules, go through the Golgi complex. Even if these are bad experiences, or sad things that happened and you are unaware of, Golgi is in charge to transfer that information to your cells. Things like rape, death, vices, sin, etc. This means that at any given moment that gene that is inactive can be activated; even if it is not active, it doesn't mean that the information is not there, or that it is dead, what happens is that it is like a ghost, hidden waiting for the "right" moment to be activated in your life and later in your generations if you don't succeed in your efforts of perfecting your genetics.

It is very interesting that according to scientists, Golgi is a chemical by which genes are turned on or off, but really, if you consider that the raw material from which you are made is spiritual, then that chemical, in the spiritual world are the temptations that the enemy is suddenly throwing into your life, because the temptations are not insignificant to your person, It is not my intention in offending you, perhaps you are a very correct person, however let me teach you what the Bible says about temptations :

1 Corinthians 10:13 *(ASV) There hath no temptation taken you but such as man can bear...*

Even though the one that presents the temptation is not human, our enemy, is a spiritual entity, but he can use physical things to present temptation, the enemy won't waste resources, he will send the "right" thing for you to fall since he knows there is a receptor in you. However, the same Bible verse gives us hope:

1 Corinthians 10:13 *(ASV) ...but God is faithful, who will not suffer you to be tempted above that ye are able; but will with the temptation make also the way of escape, that ye may be able to endure it.*

This means that temptation attacks your humanity and if there is something chemical that can awaken a gene, then the enemy will try to alter that chemical, therefore temptation will reach three areas.

Temptation manipulates chemicals in the brain through dopamine, which is a neurotransmitter that makes you feel pleasure. For example, when you smell a food that you like, in that moment there is dopamine being released in your brain. When you hold hands with your spouse, there is dopamine as well, etc. Temptation alters chemicals like dopamine, and if you don't manage to deactivate temptation through the ministration of the soul, the gene that is deactivated will be activated and it can take you to the same ending as your ancestors.

Temptation manipulates imagination, in such a way that it may be that someone begins to imagine the pleasure they are feeling in the dopamine that has already been manipulated with the temptation and then imagines things that are kept secret. If it is a problem in the sexual area, you can plot anything because as it is happening only in your brain, you are not ashamed of everything you could imagine.

Next thing that alters is the heart and its magnetic field. You need to keep in consideration that the heart's magnetic field is stronger than the mind's; in such a way that if the heart stores that information, it will prepare scenarios in which two people with the same activated gene, through epigenetics, can have an encounter and the heart's magnetic field could be a connection with the mind of the person next to them, even without saying any words.

Therefore, I insist that you need a counselor and what I mean with the word "counselor" is a person that is trained to do ministration of the soul, to take into consideration that the enemy knows the power that temptation has over us and the destruction that it can cause, reducing self-control in the person. While these things are kept hidden, the ability to withstand temptation is reduced. The more we hide sin or temptation, it will be less likely for us to withstand temptation. But if we look for help through ministration, this gene could be deactivated and epigenetics won't affect us and the blood of Christ will continue its work regenerating us, until all the ancestral data will be deleted from our genes.

The classification of the information and experiences you have is mediated by the vesicles.

When proteins bind to the appropriate receptor in the vesicle, they are encoded and transported there. If you isolate a cell from the human body, you can extract volumes of information and predict years of experience that a person has had throughout their life. That is, they are encoded, as engraved and ready to pass the information on to the next generation.

The Epigenetic Contaminations

This is only understood from the genetics (epigenetics) perspective, beyond genetics. Although now from what is known as "Epigenetics, far beyond genetics an orthodox idea of genetics, as an example: where do your battles come from? Or how many years have you been battling with the same issues? The answer, based on epigenetics, is that they didn't start with you; they just continued with you. That's the long-term impact of the family havoc.

1.- GENETICS AND EPIGENETICS

Your parents, grandparents, and great grandparent's lives could directly affect your wellbeing even though it wasn't you who experienced directly what they experienced. In other words, even though you didn't contaminate directly with the things your ancestors were contaminated, it can affect your life. Before we believed that whatever you did with your life would only affect you directly, but your genes will stay contamination-free, however, God has allowed us to have more knowledge,
revelation in order for us to know what was unknown to us before. It is important that each time that you eat the bread and drink the wine, which represents the flesh and blood of our Lord Jesus Christ, you know that the divine memory is replacing whatever is inside you so from that
moment on there will be a new beginning.

2.- CLASSIC GENETICS

In the classic genetics, your parents and grandparents simply transferred genes to you; the experiences they lived in their lives are never inherited (they are lost forever) as genes are passed unchanged from generation to generation (in a manner that the biology of inheritance was reassuring).

3.- EPIGENETICS

You are not a simple sum of genes, your decisions and lifestyle could affect your generations, something else was transferred through DNA from generation to generation. If someone inherited physical attributes from their grandparents and that makes them feel superior, it is better for that person to worry about the bad experiences of their grandparents because that's also stored in the genes and those could be activated at any given time, or even worse, that situation could be transferred to the next generations until someone decides to break with that.

This is why someone could suddenly feel protective about the things of God's, shame for what he/she has done wrong even without knowledge, can be remembering those things and feel bad about them. Thank God you and me have had the opportunity to experience an spiritual and biological regeneration.

EPIGENETICS IS:

1. The memory of a fact that's transferred from generation to generation.

2. To be connected in a hidden world (what you haven't seen in 100 or 200 years, but it is stored as experiences within you).

3. Connect todays generations with future generations.

4. Epigenetics is not what you eat, but what your parents and grandparents ate.

5. Environmental contaminations from ancestors that can cause diseases in their grandchildren even though they were not literally exposed, this includes the spiritual environments.

6. The genetic imprint; genes that keep memories of their origins. Genes have a memory that you can't imagine, but it is activated depending on the environments that may surround you.

Before the fall of mankind, Golgi transferred information coming from God from one generation to another generation because this information was the only existing information available to the humanity God had created.

Psalms 145:4 *(New King James Version)*
4 One generation shall praise Your works

Los Ancestros

to another, and shall declare Your mighty acts.

After the fall, this continues working the same way, but now transferring INIQUITY.

How to Break Epigenetics?

If not because God has been revealing this to us, you could think at any point that what you're fighting against right now is something without explanation. Therefore, I present you the following genetics chart:

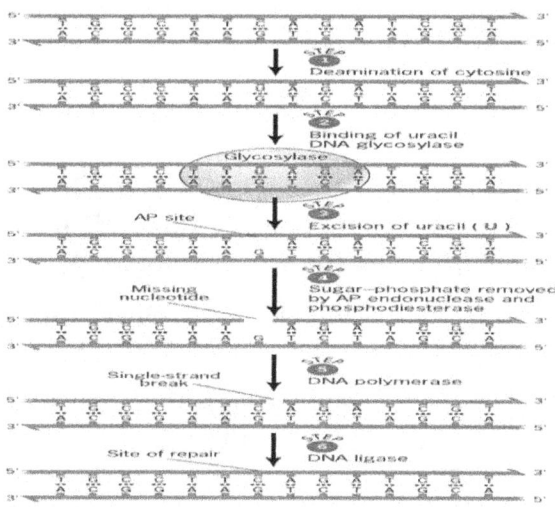

The green is a cell that supervises all your genetics, the one that finds errors, in a way that when those are found, it edits them. If you have allowed Jesus' blood to enter your body through the Holy Supper, you have a cell from the Lord which is enough to change your DNA completely. But I want to focus on the chart and show you the first data line, it is your original DNA. This is the genetics without alterations; the next line is not the same, it has a "U" in red showing an error; the cell that is presented in green is showing what is marked will alter its development; in other words, that's the negative influence that a person can have. I'll describe the process of the area with damage and how to correct it:

DNA REPAIR

There are some mechanisms to repair DNA:

- In the diagram you can observe in the first row a normal DNA, a double helix: an object having a three-dimensional shape like that of a wire wound uniformly in a single layer around a cylinder or cone, as in a spiral staircase.
- The rows are united by the pairing of the nitrogenous bases that form the DNA.
- The pairing of the nitrogenous bases is specific.

Los Ancestros

- If there is a wrong pairing, DNA is damaged or becomes a different one with distinct functions.
- The wrong pairing could happen due to an external damage or simply because the wrong nitrogenous bases united (unequal yoke).
- In the chart, the first step (step 1) the base C is transformed into U. This was a change due to an external thing. This is damaging the DNA.
- Step 2 has an enzyme called glycosylase DNA, it finds the pairing error or the DNA damage. The enzyme checks the DNA till it finds an error or damage (this is called the revision).
- The enzyme gets united with the damage segmentation and cuts it and extracts it creating a space in the sequence (step 3 y 4).
- There is another enzyme that helps creating this space and is called endonuclease (step 4).
- Steps 5 and 6, show that the DNA enzyme polymerase and ligase fill the space that was created in the sequence of the correct DNA.

- Using it as a model, the DNA sequence that was healthy.
- Remembering David's example, that was recorded on Psalm 51, I could say that the genetic errors are found through revelation.
- The Holy Spirit is the enzyme that finds the error and lets us know.
- Confessing our sins is what cuts the segmentation and the Holy Supper is the method that forms a new DNA having as a model Christ's DNA, in a way that our DNA gets edited to be like it was originally intended under a perspective of perfection so you get to have Christ's genetics.

Based on this explanation, I can say then that this is how ancestral diseases and anything negative start; That is why the Bible says, he who is in Christ is a new creation, old things have passed away, all are made new. But then the question arises: when can genetics be negatively altered? It is deformed in different ways, one of them is the following:

UNEQUAL YOKE

The wrong pairing or matching can occur due to external damage or simply because two wrong nitrogenous bases are united (unequal yoke).

2 Corinthians 6:14 *(NLT) Do not be unequally bound together with unbelievers. For what partnership can righteousness have with lawlessness? Or what fellowship can light have with darkness?*

1 Corinthians 7:15 *(NLT) But if the unbelieving partner leaves, let him leave. In such cases the brother or sister is not bound. But God has called us to peace.*

Generational faith is a matter of epigenetics. The question therefore is, when does this happen?

Breaking Epigenetics

1 Corinthians 11:24-25 *(AMP) And when He had given thanks, He broke it and said, "This is My body, which is for you. Do this in remembrance of Me." In the same way, after supper He took the cup, saying, "This cup is the new covenant in My blood; do this, as often as you drink it, in remembrance of Me."*

It is necessary that each Christian give the Holy Supper a higher level of importance; sadly, some have it as a ritual, as something empty that has no repercussion, ignoring that each time we participate, God invites us to His table and it is an opportunity to regenerate our DNA.

What Does Memory Mean?

Remember that the body has memory; the blood has memory which affects the body, be it in a positive or negative way. It is interesting that when you look in the Gospels for the moment of the Lord's Supper, Mark and Matthew do not refer to memory. It is the Gospel of Luke that does it because he was a doctor, he had another perspective regarding what the blood represents, which the Apostle Paul receives by revelation that there is memory in the blood and in the body, that is why the above quote points to the word memory twice.

The word MEMORY comes from the Greek medical term identified in the Strong's Dictionary with the code G364; and it means: medical history. This is generated by the patient itself, therefore when someone goes to a doctor, they have to answer the questions asked by the doctor because the doctor needs this information to know if this is a simple pain or if it can be an inherited disease. Obviously, it is of utmost importance to answer with the truth, even when we feel ashamed of something; it is the same way with ministration, we have to be truthful so the DNA correction will be accurate.

For this reason, when you participate in the Lord's Supper, you cannot do it without understanding and have the elements in your hand only to fill out a religious protocol. You must know the power that you can reach because in the body and blood of the Lord there is memory, in such a way that when you get closer to the Lord you can tell the Him what your ailments are, including ancestral ones.

Not only physical ailments, but even in matters of the soul because a difficult economic situation can cause illness in anyone, especially when it is due to ancestral inheritance, because the person may be doing everything in their power to straighten out their economy, but as it is an ancestral curse that It is directly affecting their economy, it will not be able to be straightened out until the Lord enters to restore spiritual genetics.

This will not happen until the code that was deformed, the Lord edits it to leave it restored to its original state, that is, perfect.

When I talk about spiritual genetics that need to be regenerated, I'm talking about the raw material of a person, because once the spiritual DNA is regenerated, it will have repercussions in its physical DNA and the restoration will be completed.

2 Corinthians 5:17 *(AMP) Therefore if anyone is in Christ he is a new creature; the old things have passed away. Behold, new things have come.*

Take your children, grandchildren and great grandchildren into consideration, whatever they inherit is not their fault, but today you could break with all of that. Remember, all the ancestral spiritual or physical curses can be broken in the name of Jesus Christ, before these things manifest in them. Maybe it is embarrassing to recognize some of these things, but it will be worse if your generations go through things because you didn't take the opportunity to break with these things when you had the opportunity.

Even worse, if at any given time in the past you had a wicked lifestyle, that changed your epigenetics in a negative way, but when you decided to serve Christ, you are allowing Him to begin with a new edition, a positive one, of your epigenetics, to be transferred to your generations. Of course, it is the blood of Christ the one that makes these changes, the ministration of the soul also helps shortening the process of deliverance, but there are other things that you also must learn so when you experience them you can take advantage of them

Chapter 4

The Transformation

Mario & Luz Rivera

I will begin by saying that the purpose of this teaching is for you to achieve understanding regarding to the things that are inside you, it is necessary for you to be able to discern in a way that you will pursue transformation through Jesus' blood (therefore be perfected). In previous chapters I've mentioned that there are people out there sinning and making mistakes intentionally using the false statement "nobody's perfect" as an excuse to continue living the same way their parents (ancestors) lived. But according to the Bible, God wants you to advance in the pursuit of knowing Him more, to be more like Him (perfect). This is the reason why this chapter is titled "Transformation", since our main focus will be a metamorphosis (which means: to transform). What we're aiming for is a transformation in our genetics to get rid of the negative and achieve the positive from God.

You also need to know that the word TRANSFORMATION is not only connected with the word metamorphosis, but also to these 6 words:

1. Transformation: Metamorphoo #3339. Romans 12:2

2. Transformation: Metachemita-zo #3345. Philippians 3:21 (Positive and negative)

3. Transformation: Metaballo #3328. Acts 28:6

4. Transformation: Haphak #2015. 1 Samuel 10:6

5. Transformation: Muwr #4171. Jeremiah 48:11

6. Transformation: Allaso #236. 1 Corinthians 15:51-52, 2 Corinthians 3:18

– This last one happens when the rapture occurs, it is one regarding the body.

– Without all of these, we won't experience the "Allaso Transformation".

1 Corinthians 15:51-52 (NASB) Behold, I tell you a mystery; we will not all sleep, but we will all be changed, in a moment, in the twinkling of an eye, at the last trumpet; for the trumpet will sound, and the dead will be raised imperishable, and we will be changed.

There is a transformation that only can be accomplished by the power of God, taking into consideration that the **transformation** described in the previous verse will only take 11 milliseconds.

However, when it comes to metamorphosis, this is part of the evolution process of a living being, it will happen at any moment, otherwise it will be like being trapped in an involute cycle. As for you and me, He created and placed within each of His children, laws that function inherently and that those laws had their own constitution, in such a way that if you comply with what the law says, the constitution will bless you. However, when the principle of that law is violated, the person inherently destroys himself, a situation that is still in force, for example:

The first man put in the Garden, the Lord left a fountain to serve as life; In fact, the Bible says that there was a tree from which, when he ate, it made his years last, man at that time was not eternal because he depended on that source, it was the tree of life. Unlike the tree from which he was forbidden to eat, this was the tree of the knowledge of good and evil. But he was disobedient even though consequences were declared when eating it.

At that time something that man did not have entered his genetics; the death gene. That's why the Bible says that sin entered through a man and death through sin; therefore all have sinned; hence, epigenetically-mind came to affect all mankind, not only to the inclination of sin but to the point of reaching death.

About 10 years ago, I wrote a book related to genes and I talked about the death gene. Just like this book, I also based on genetic studies where geneticists were doing research to carry out what was called the biblical genome, the book of life.

With years of research several geneticists got together with the purpose of putting each one their best effort, experience, academic knowledge and discovered how human genetics work in say they knew everything about how humans to the point of knowing how to create a human being and predict its weaknesses, illnesses, strengths, even death.

During that time, many of these geneticists said they were surprised by the fact that there was a gene that seemed (younger) than the rest. It looked like it was placed after the rest had already been there for a while, but there it was, as part of the DNA. This gene even showed that there was a dependency between it with other genes in the sequence chain and this gene is the "death" gene. In other words, when mankind was created, death wasn't part of the plan, therefore death is not part of your plan.

All of these and more information is part of a book I wrote titled: THE GENETICS OF THE ADAMS. I described then the **Mitochondrion** and how mitochondrion is "the mother of all living", the interesting thing about this is that that was what Adam called Eve.

According to geneticists, we all have that gene and it's connecting us to "our mother", sadly that mother sinned and all her offspring has that gene altered under the perspective of that sin. It is also interesting to understand that this gene called "the death gene," this was a consequence of Adam's disobedience.

Connected with this information, and what I taught previously (chapters 1, 2 and 3), according to new research, DNA can be edited. This was discovered recently, however, God had already spoken to us about it through His word, because we know we can edit our genetics through Jesus' powerful blood. This is why we need to keep in mind that when Jesus came to earth to shed his blood on the cross, that blood is was the element of redemption and regeneration.

This is the key to the metamorphosis or transformation, this is why we use the word REGENERATION, your genetics will be restored, and your genes will go back to their original state of perfection, why? Because God doesn't want you to live under the influence of negative genetics.

Now, the purpose this teaching is for you to know the principles of how all of these work, for you to have the necessary maturity and responsibility to ask God to show you what needs to be transformed in you. It is true that we all come from different backgrounds, but we all have in common that we all have genetics, maybe with different needs, but in the end we all have the need to be transformed by God.

It may be that you do not have the ability to investigate all that ancestral background which in one way or another is in everyone; that is why it is the Holy Spirit who reveals what must be edited in your DNA. I say this because it may be that someone comes from a long-lived family and may even had the opportunity to ask their great-grandfather about what he knows about his ancestors.

But when the biological parents are no longer present, it is more difficult to find out what were the weaknesses of all that group of people from whom you come.

Epigenetics can transform genetics, if there are experiences or things that were done that marked your genes, you have hope,

God will change you. It is necessary to understand that this happens because there are memories that were stored in your genes, ready to be activated at any given time. How do you know what these memories are? If you can't ask someone from your family, you can ask God to reveal it to you, as it happened with David.

That's the only way you will know what your epigenetics heritage is. Hence the idea of being supervised to see if you are working in order to reduce it, break it and change it; that is PERFECTING THE GENETICS, but as long as you don't change it, that is iniquity as David said:

Psalm 51:5 (KJV) *Behold, I was shapen in iniquity...*

Nobody plans to live in iniquity, you have to proyect blessings over your life, however a situation might come to light and you will know that it has affected your life, this same way it will affect your offspring.

This is precisely why you must find out what are the things you inherited, in order to fight against them and not transfer them to your generations by receiving the revelation about these things. In order to have the opportunity to be free and correct your genes in the name of Jesus; in fact, if no genetic disrupt has manifested in your life, you can start asking God today for Him to regenerate your DNA before anything that may harm you may occur.

The Ghost in Genetics

The same verse in Psalms lets us see the importance of REVELATION when it comes to the GHOST in our GENETICS (INIQUITY), and to be able to understand where your struggles come from, starting with the way of living you can adapt as part of the process.

1. If you decide to live in a different way (not the same way as your parents lived but according God's will), this could change your genetics inherited by your parents, grandparents, and even great grandparents.

2. If even after asking Jesus into your heart, you decide to live the same way as your ancestors did, this could affect your offspring even if they don't do the same things you did.

THE EPIGENETICS GHOST is a situation that you don't even know specifically what it is, but it is something and acts under ancestral information.

David's Genetics Ghost

What the parents do, affects their children, for example: David receives the experiences that where encoded in him and affected him and his offspring, so you must consider the following:

1. DAVID'S PAST
   It is the result of 10 previous generations, how? Judah sexually involved with Tamar (Genesis 38:13-18).
2. DAVID'S PRESENT David's ancestral problem manifests in the same area; sexual; transferring it to his generations, as a bridge (2 Samuel 12).
3. DAVID'S FUTURE The sexual problems that David's sons manifested, were manifested in Absalom when he raped David's concubines and when Amnon raped his sister Tamar (2 Samuel 13:10-15), it also manifested in Solomon since he had 1000 women.

This is what is known as epigenetics and the bible teaches us that it means: "the long-term impact of family ravages". However, many Christians in a fundamentalist way (many times with good intentions) think that when they come to Christ and all problems end and from that point forward everything will just "automatically" work, and this couldn't be further from reality. Even though someone could have a lot of faith, we all need to go through the regeneration path, nobody changes overnight and nobody can fulfill the calling of holiness and consecration overnight, it needs to be the same way as when a baby is born.

The baby doesn't have an intellectual memory, but the baby has neuronal memory (which is different). This baby has a memory ready to be filled, intellectually and lifestyle (the one that the baby's parents have) whether it is a positive or a negative one and this is especially important the first two years of life. The baby is acquiring those first two years 50% of the information that will determine his/her personality.

If a child is raised with restrictions or manipulations, this child will have serious issues as an adult. It is the same way when we are born again in Christ, God is allowing you to fill up with sound doctrine, and you must take advantage of this, in order for you to reach the level of a new creation.

This is the why in the spiritual jurisdiction for a new believer hell is no longer a problem, but the entanglements of life. The bible allows us to see that the sin of the unrepentant parent makes their generations carry negative effects and opens doors for their generations to struggle with phobias, anxiety, sexual weakness, depression, etc., Even people who serve at church could be experiencing this, because they have not yet been able to experience total freedom, their issues are in their DNA and only God can access that and edit their DNA from all error operation from darkness.

Deuteronomy 5:9 *(ESV) "You shall not bow down to them or serve them; for I the LORD your God am a jealous God, visiting the iniquity of the fathers on the children to the third and fourth generation of those who hate me ..."*

When you do research on the word *"visiting"* it is a Hebrew word identified with the code H6485 in the Strong's Concordance and it allows us to clearly see that God will visit your life to see if you are working to get rid of the iniquity inherited from your ancestors until it is completely eliminated from your life. There are times when God visits you with His divine "measuring tape" to see if the iniquity is decreasing or if you got comfortable with it.

When God sees that the iniquity is decreasing, He allows you to realize how to work towards that goal so you keep on advancing, because it is different to receive iniquity as an inheritance than producing it to pass it on to your generations and it can increase instead of decreasing.

You need to keep in mind that iniquity causes iniquity, not sin. Taking into consideration that iniquity is the strength to sin, you could say that it adds up and the enemy takes advantage of this to increase his influence in you and your generations.

It is interesting to see that the phrase *"visiting the iniquity of the fathers on the children"* appears five times in the bible:

1. Deuteronomy 5:9.

2. Exodus 20:5.

3. Exodus 34:7.

4. Numbers 14:18.

5. Jeremiah 32:18.

This topic is very important for you to understand. I will continue to talk about some definitions and concepts that will help you understanding it in a better way, not just its importance, but its origin:

GENE: Is found in the chromosomes (in each chromosome there is diversity of genes) and these determine the character.

GENETICS: Studies the phenomenon of inheritance, variation, similarities and differences, principles and causes, it can even determine the number of days of a person, as a consequence it can be determine when a person will die.

GENEALOGY: The ancestors of each individual.

What do you get from them?

• You need to investigate: what happened with them?

• How did their soul get contaminated?

• How did they acquire deformities in their bones, flesh, organs (heart, kidneys, etc.) even their senses.

• How did they fall in sin and iniquity?

God is allowing this topic to be studied because it is extremely important and you need to understand it, you must fight with whatever is disrupting your DNA, in order to break free from all these situations that have been bothering you for so long.

When the Human Genome was discovered, the information was kept for a while since it could be used for good or evil, since in your genes you could even see how long you're going to live, so if someone wanted to get a life insurance, the first thing the insurance company would do is to run a blood test to see if it was profitable or not for them to sell that insurance; even for someone applying for a job, they could run a test to measure the person's intelligence since intelligence (and the lack of it) are inherited.

This is something science discovered recently, but it was written in the bible a long time ago.

Psalms 139:16 *(NIV) your eyes saw my unformed body; all the days ordained for me were written in your book before one of them came to be.*

The genetic codes are written in the book of life and God is allowing these to be discovered now, in the end times, in order for each one of our DNAs to achieve total freedom.

The Epigenetic Behavior and Destiny

Behavior, what we decide to do in life, actions and decisions are linked to our behavior and this to our epigenetics which will decide the destiny of each person (despite predestination); remember that you were pre-destined by God and He asks you for His will to be done in your life.

He won't force you for this to happen, however, what you decide to do will show if you are being influenced by that pre-destination or if you decide to do something else.

The problem is that you're not only influencing your life, but also your offspring, in a way that if you decide to walk the path you shouldn't walk, this will impact the lives of your generations and when Jesus presents Himself to them as the way the truth and the life, their hearts might be hardened due to the decisions you made.

If you decided to follow Jesus, your epigenetics heritage will help your generations' hearts to be tender and willing to invite Christ into their lives.

When you do something GOD or BAD, in that moment, inside your body, your genes start working as a response of what you just did. Every time your brain gives the order to do something, your genes begin working to modify your genetics and record that new behavior.

Taking into consideration that I'm not talking about evil spirits or demons that are acting in you or against you, but this is something that happens naturally in the genetics law. When you behave badly or poorly, your tolerance levels increase, in other words, people could be sinning and the Spirit wouldn't convict them from their sin; they will be able to do bad things and not feel sad or bad about it, because of that decision that they made and acted on; of course, when you do good things, you also make your genes change your genetics for good and every time it will be better until it's perfect, it is like developing a skill.

When a dad makes the decision to obey Christ, that action positively affects his children, to the point that if he decides to follow Christ, his offspring might develop gifts that they did not get from their father. When God sees a father following Him, out of mercy He gives spiritual gifts to him and his children. Everything can change due to that decision, due to one man, his generations will be re-programmed (regenerated) with God's guidance and they will have the original design and will be able to be perfected. The problem is when you do bad things, because the sperm and ovum are also genetically infected in order for your generations to keep on doing things that are not right. That is why it is necessary to pray, bless and prophesy to the sons and daughters that were begotten before the father and mother were Christians. Because it is the responsibility of the parents that they have inherited what they have inherited, even without much knowledge, it is still the responsibility of the parents. Remember that the Bible clearly says:

Hosea 4:6 *(NIV) my people are destroyed from lack of knowledge. "Because you have rejected knowledge, I also reject you as my priests; because you have ignored the law of your God, I also will ignore your children.*

God wants to transfer His knowledge, the problem is that many don't want to receive that knowledge even when it means to keep (negatively) affecting their generations.

Abraham had an opportunity to do so and he took advantage of it:

Genesis 17:1 *(ASV) And when Abram was ninety years old and nine, Jehovah appeared to Abram, and said unto him, I am God Almighty; walk before me, and be thou perfect.*

Abraham came from a polytheistic culture, he was from a region where they worshiped different gods, his previous generations were esoteric, until God told him to leave his house, his family, and his land. God gave him the opportunity to decide and take action, Abraham was not perfect he was contaminated by the things people around him did however, God changed that.

Abraham changed his ways so from that day forward he could be aware of his actions and he was able to begin a new breed, a perfect one. This is what God is asking you today, for Him to work in your life from now to eternity, from what you are now to what your generations can become.

Epigenetics is not only what your genes have transferred to you, but also what you can transfer to your generations. You are not just the sum of 42 people but many more. You can see that there is not only genetics but also epigenetics and there is information in your genes that can get activated also reprogrammed.

In the previous chapter I presented this charts:

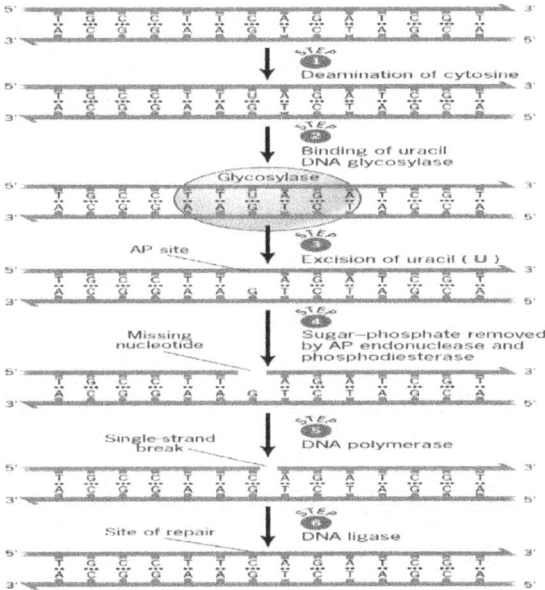

Maybe I'm insisting in some points, but I do it because I consider it to be of utmost importance. In the first series you can see the representation of genes the way God design them; the line that looks like a **U** in red, represents a genetic error, which could also be a malformation, illness or negative influence. When geneticists find a genetic error, they know that this person will have a complicated life (health related).

When you see the third series of genes, you can see a part that is in a pale green color, this is showing you the error, it is precisely what a cell does; it is supervising so by the time there is error, it can be edited to be able to remove that **U** and cut it and insert what should appear in that place and do the respective reparation. This is what is known as excision repair. That cell is Jesus' blood.

The Genetic Repair By Excision

Your thoughts change your genetics.
Your thoughts also continuously affect your genes, which need to be transformed over time to match your cell mechanisms with the expectations that you have and the experiences you've lived.

1. Create Memories.

2. Feelings.

3. Expectations.

4. Ideas.

5. Plans.

6. Projects, etc.

Everything is encoded.

It is important to know that what I listed before, when you do it in a negative way, will seriously affect your genetics. These things have been seen as an emotional problem and that's accurate, but it is worse to have memories of negative thoughts because it will affect your genetics. This is why God at some point had to destroy humanity, because they were not correcting themselves, so they had to be destroyed:

***Genesis 6:5-7** (NASB) Then the LORD saw that the wickedness of man was great on the earth, and that every intent of the thoughts of his heart was only evil continually. The LORD was sorry that He had made man on the earth, and He was grieved in His heart. The LORD said, "I will blot out man whom I have created from the face of the land, from man to animals to creeping things and to birds of the sky; for I am sorry that I have made them." 8But Noah found favor in the eyes of the LORD.*

God saw that the epigenetics of that humanity was damaged, they damaged it with bad thoughts, they were not willing to change, it was better to wipe them from the face of the earth. This allows us to see that when we keep "hoarding" bad moments (memories) it is self-destructive and you are damaging your genes and it will seriously affect your generations. How does it work? Bad moments (memories) get you in a bad mood, developing bad temper, it makes you hate, etc., and this directly affects your generations, it will affect your children, it is like you're planting seeds of hate in them, seeds of bitterness, pain, resentment, etc.

The Dna's Metamorphosis

If your thoughts change, it is because the neurotransmitters have changed (chemicals in the brain).

If the neurotransmitters are changed, it is because its reproduction changed (where the chemicals of the thoughts are produced).

If the production of neurotransmitters changes, it is because the genes changed.

If you reject your bad memories, bad thoughts, bad projects, resentment, you're submitting your genetics to Jesus' transformation and He will take you to the process to reach perfection. Everything that you think about, good or bad, will become part of your epigenetics.

Romans 12:2 *(NIV) Do not conform to the pattern of this world, but be transformed by the renewing of your mind. Then you will be able to test and* *approve what God's will is--his good, pleasing and perfect will.*

I can then say that you need to try your best to change your way of thinking, by doing this, you're changing your DNA. You also need to know that one of the things that damage your epigenetics is preconceived ideas you have (prejudices). Anticipating things you don't know will happen, because they are damaging your genes in advance without knowing what will happen, but there are some people who are renewing their mind:

Titus 1:15 *(NIV) To the pure, all things are pure, but to those who are corrupted and do not believe, nothing is pure. In fact, both their minds and consciences are corrupted.*

GENETICS' CHANGED BY FOOD

What you eat can change your genetic code because it can turn your genes **off** or **on** and this is transmitted from one generation to the next. This is something people did not understand when Jesus was on earth and they missed the opportunity to experience the change of life they needed:

John 6:51 *(NIV) "I am the living bread that came down from heaven. Whoever* *eats this bread will live forever. This bread is my flesh, which I will give for the life of the world."*

John 6:54-56 *(NASB) "He who eats My flesh and drinks My blood has eternal life, and I will raise him up on the last day. "For My flesh is true food, and My blood is true drink. "He who eats My flesh and drinks My blood abides in Me, and I in him. "As the living Father sent Me, and I live because of the Father, so he who eats Me, he also will live because of Me. 58"This is the bread which came down out of heaven; not as the fathers ate and died; he who eats this bread will live forever."*

John 6:66 *(NIV) From this time many of his disciples turned back and no longer followed him.*

You can see that Jesus gave them the opportunity of a lifetime, they had already recognized Him as their Lord and savior they even walked with Him (this is why they were called "His disciples"), however, when the time came to change their DNA and delete all ancestral iniquity, they decided to continue with their old lifestyle.

Today with what I'm writing here, insisting many times on some specific things you have the opportunity to have a new beginning; the change you were looking for, fighting the problem from the root in order for you to be a blessing to others and to be able to teach others through God's revelation that He has sent us to know in the end of times.

CHAPTER 5
GOD'S (YHVH) GENETICS AND ENGINEERING

I cannot deny that genetics are an engineering of God, I can say this because of the abundant words that the Bible shows us related with this subject. I have been repeating this on several occasions, how it is that God was in charge of attracting attention through His word using terms like, GENERATIONS, DESCENDANTS, SEED, CHILDREN, PROLE, etc.

All of this is intimately linked to what I have been teaching. I am referring to GENETICS. In such a way that if it is an engineering of God, which it is; The intention is that each believer, at the time of reproducing will transfer, the work of God to the next generation in order to continue seeking and calling God. Based on the fact that genetics are an influence when inherited from our ancestors whether for good or not, their influence will affect what a person will and will not do.

That is why Satan launches attacks at that genetic angle, Satan saw that the purpose of God's engineering is to transmit His work to the next generations; then by simple logic he thought that in the same way he could manage to degenerate everything while it was transmitted from one generation to another with the purpose that the inheritance were diseases, sins, iniquities, etc. Then the moment came when the Father, Based on His divine plan, sends the Son to come with His pure genetics, without blemish, a perfect genetic in order that through His genetics you can be rescued and transformed and become the candidate to inaugurate the new Earth. On what basis do I say this?

New Breed

2 Corinthians 5:17 *(New Century Version)* *17 If anyone belongs to Christ, there is a new creation. The old things have **gone**; everything is made new!*

A very good way of saying things is by saying that old things are passing away, here they are all made new. Of course, by faith you can declare the literalness of this verse, however I cannot deny that it is a process in which old things will finally pass, as you learn, understand, mature and reach perfection, this is a Biblical truth.

In such a way that they pass, although in the previous verse it refers to the past tense, because as I repeat to you, by faith you believe that God has already done it and it is He who sees you that way too.

We Live for The Next Generation

This is why during all that you have been reading, you noticed that I carried a very important point, which is the fact of becoming aware that you are being prepared to live in the next generation; which is why God is revealing all of this to us. Unfortunately, I cannot say the same about your ancestors because they were unaware of many things, which is why they were victims of the inheritances they received from their ancestors.

They did not have the blessings that you are receiving; but consider that this preparation can be progressive, as degenerative, depending on what you decide today and at this time, obviously you also live for the positive preparation that you will give to your future descendants.

***1 Peter 1:18-19** (World English Bible) [18] knowing that you were redeemed, not with corruptible things, with silver or gold, from the useless way of life handed down from your fathers, [19] but with precious blood, as of a lamb without blemish or spot, the blood of Christ.*

Investigating what it may mean, WITHOUT BLEMISH AND WITHOUT SPOT, I can say that it is where the concept of what is PERFECT fits, that is why it speaks of the blood of Christ which is perfect and the only one that can purify your genes contaminated from any situation.

Now, the application of blood has a principle that was considered as a legal law, it is what you know as the New Covenant. However, for this New Covenant there was a substitution of a covenant. This covenant had repercussions on the genes by a better covenant which only the Lord Jesus Christ can offer.

Apply the same principle within the same legal law of substitution; Jesus died for you, he descended into the lake of fire to suffer the second death and with that you would be completely replaced, but, you must also consider a very important point which is, that although it is true the Lord substitutes your blood for His, He will not mix both bloods.

There must first be a recognition of all the negative that can be in you through an inheritance and you must reject and to surrender it to the Lord. Once all of this has come to light, the blood of Jesus can then enter and operate the DNA of the Lord instead of yours. A decision you must make for yourself.

The Bible mentions at least five times that the Lord will visit the iniquity of the parents and their children up to third and fourth generations. To this topic I have explained that when the Lord said he would visit iniquity, in the Hebrew language this word clearly states that the Lord supervises whether a person is working to reduce the level of iniquity that one has inherited from his/her ancestors.

Also, if one has truly given this the importance it deserves once God has revealed the origin of some of the problems which you are unable to find the reason for. Meanwhile you are working to nullify the same problems in order for your descendants will not inherit. One more time, I want to remind you that inheritances do not only come from parents, grandparents, great grandparents but also through epigenetics.

This is the accumulation of an inheritance of at least 42 generations ago, from which you can have genetic information ready to be transferred to your descendants, be this characters, diseases, visions and many more things, even inheriting lived experiences that they can be encrypted in a cell and available to be manifested at the least expected moment.

The Golgi apparatus

Once again, I will refer to Golgi, I have said that this is the vehicle that contains all the information and ancestral history that one can possess. This Golgi is in charge of bringing this information from generation to generation. It is also in charge of feeding the DNA's molecule with all this information. Now, understanding all this, you can say that the history of the soul of each one, dates from many more years than what you can get to live on this Earth.

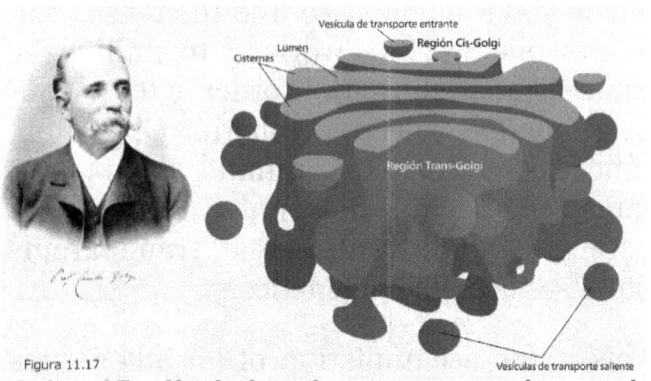

Figura 11.17

Scientifically it has been proven that as in the biological aspect as in the physical DNA and the soul a lot of ancestral information is stored there. An example was seen some time ago, when a person condemned to a death sentence by the so-called lethal injection; survived and while he was convulsing, they took him for tests using sophisticated devices, they were able to see the battle that person was having in their imagination.

They then discovered that this individual was a descendant of warriors who existed approximately 400 years ago and was a descendant of that tribe. They managed to penetrate his imagination and presented him with scenarios where he had to fight to survive, thus achieving his goal in the face of what he was seeing in his imagination, but all that was an effect of what he had accumulated in his soul.

Biologically speaking, this is the same scenario. There can be a positive or negative influence according to the lifestyle of your parents, it could even be that you could be winning battles that your parents were never able to overcome, including situations that quickly turned negative but your faith gave you a victory. And now you are the one winning this battle in order for them to end.

This is why you must know about these topics in order not to enter the spiritual warfare in ignorance but to enter with God's knowledge and in faith in Him. With the power of the blood of Jesus Christ. I say all this because the Golgi apparatus was is in charge of transferring all that information, which worked according to the purposes of God before the fall of Adam; it continues to function, but the information it transmits is not what God wants it to transmit, unless you dispose yourself to be perfected more and more being freed from all negative ancestral influences.

Then Golgi will transmit to the next generation, the way you sought God, how you served him and believed him and all its positive aspect. Golgi will be in charge of transmitting to your descendants in order for a story like Timothy will emerge. Timothy of whom the Bible says he had a mother of faith because he also had a grandmother of faith. Inclusive the love with which you obey the Lord and believe him you will also have joy when you tithe and bring offerings, which you will also inherit to your descendants as Abraham did with Levi.

Golgi: The Generational Source Of Information

Every person is designed by God to fulfill their purpose and each person has the capability to visualize their future genetically speaking. The purpose was encoded in the DNA and in the Golgi apparatus, which is in charge of transmitting that information to your generations. However, at the fall of humanity this was disrupted and now it only transmits "iniquity," for this reason the need of deliverance through the blood of Christ is needed. Even though I have mentioned it before, I want to bring to remembrance a very important point which this verse shows us

Psalm 145:4 (Amplified Bible) *4 One generation shall praise Your works to another, and shall declare Your mighty and remarkable acts.*

God designed a genetic engineering to transfer the accumulation of an ancestral inheritance of blessings, but with the fall of humanity, mankind began to transmit iniquity; although it had been designed to work properly in transferring genes and forming nations, known as generations. This is why you must think that you do not live only for yourself and that your experiences are yours alone; what you do, good or bad, is stored to serve future generations.

Parent's Iniquity

God's original plan was to prosper us and give us a better future. This was lost in human cells when sin entered humanity. God knew what His plan was for humanity, the need of redemption with new blood, in order to correctly restore genes.

1 John 1:7 (New Century Version)
7 But if we live in the light, as God is in the light, we can share fellowship with each other. Then the blood of Jesus, God's Son, cleanses us from every sin.

God sent Jesus to die on a cross, as I have said before; He shed his blood in order to cleanse genes contaminated by iniquity, which were found in the "old man."

Transferable Engineering

Because genes have the engineering capacity to transfer, you and I are responsible of what we are transferring to the next generation. For example, if you disobey God, this will influence and affect the next generation to become disobedient as well. We must be conscious of what we are transferring to our descendants and what is in our genetics.

Psalm 78:5-8 *(Revised Standard Version)*
5 He established a testimony in Jacob, and appointed a law in Israel, which he commanded our fathers to teach to their children; 6 that the next generation might know them, the children yet unborn, and arise and tell them to their children, 7 so that they should set their hope in God, and not forget the works of God, but keep his commandments; 8 and that they should not be like their fathers, a stubborn and rebellious generation, a generation whose heart was not steadfast, whose spirit was not faithful to God.

Although I have already mentioned some of this in summary form; I want to leave it as part of a topic in order for it to be considered important, although in reality everything you are reading is of the utmost importance. Now I will begin to explain about the things that should be edited in your genetics, as well as how you should do it; because I already mentioned it, genetics can be edited, I exemplified it with some graphics; now we will see it more detailed:

Repair by Excision

In the graphs I presented perfect DNA codes, you can also go back to see the graphs where a genetic alteration in a gene is clearly shown, I also showed how it is that a cell, representing the blood of Jesus, supervises that all the DNA is in the perfect order designed by God; in such a way that when finding an error, it returns to the DNA that is intact to mark the same part that is damaged in the other line and thus be able to substitute the bad for the good; that's a DNA repair or excision repair; however there are many more mechanisms to repair DNA.

SOME OF THE THINGS THAT CAN BE FOUND IN GENETICS

Below I will describe a small list of chromosomes in which the following situations can be found:

Chromosome # 1 = prostate cancer.

Chromosome # 4 = Parkinson's disease, neurological disorders (memory loss).

Chromosome # 5 = schizophrenia, insanity.

Chromosome # 7 = cystic fibrosis (breathing and digestion problem).

From what I can understand from this, is the importance of having self-dominion, with the purpose, not only to get away from those sinful things, but to be able to order the DNA to receive the genetic data of the blood of Christ. Obviously not all people have these types of situations, however the ones that do have them should know that they can take authority in the name of Jesus in order for DNA to be regenerated and return to its original state of perfection that God created. Then all the genetic disruption that someone may have, can be edited with the purpose that all the error that is producing is eliminated.

Chromosome # 11 = alcoholism, manic, depression ...

Chromosome # 21 = Mongolianism, Down syndrome ...

Chromosome # alpha 1 = smokers ...

Chromosome # X = mental retardation ...

Chromosome # Ebrca2 = breast and ovarian cancer ...

Chromosome # 2 = depression (female is the carrier in gene # 2 when depression is inherited).

New epigenetic data say there are only 30,000 genes, although traditional genetics says there are 100,000 genes; and some 3,500 genetic diseases have been discovered, thus isolating about 1,800. That is why God wants to work on the metamorphosis of genetics, the reality of things is that if a transformation is not made in genetics, there is no place for a total transformation.

This is why the Lord is allowing all this to be discovered at this time, with the purpose that all have the opportunity of a total restoration through the sacrament: the bread is the body of Christ and the wine is His blood. For this reason, if someone belittles the Lord's Supper, today is the time for them to reflect and take advantage of the opportunity that God is giving them with everything that I am teaching today. I have also taught other points where genetics can be changed:

1. **YOUR THOUGHTS CHANGE GENETICS**

    Your thoughts also continually affect the genes that must transform over time to match your cellular mechanisms with the expectations you've made for yourself and the experiences you've had.

    1. Create memories
    2. Feelings
    3. Expectations
    4. Ideas
    5. Plans

6. Projects, etc.

All this remains codified.

Genesis 6:5-7 *(Revised Standard Version)* *⁵ The* L<small>ORD</small> *saw that the wickedness of man was great in the earth, and that every imagination of the thoughts of his heart was only evil continually. ⁶ And the* L<small>ORD</small> *was sorry that he had made man on the earth, and it grieved him to his heart. ⁷ So the* L<small>ORD</small> *said, "I will blot out man whom I have created from the face of the ground, man and beast and creeping things and birds of the air, for I am sorry that I have made them."*

The Metamorphosis Of Dna

1. To change someone's way of thinking, in the physical part you have to change the synapse.
2. To change the synopsis, the neurotransmitters must be changed.
3. To change neurotransmitters you have to change the production of neurotransmitters

4. To change the production of neurotransmitters, you have to change your genes.

Therefore, when you repent of your sins, you are changing a lot of synapses or thoughts, which allow your behavior and values to change through learning because brain chemicals change. Hence then the importance of renewal in your way of thinking.

2. YOUR FOOD WILL CHANGE GENETICS

What you eat can change the genetic code for your heirs, turn genes off or on, and that off gene is then passed from one generation to the next.

John 6:51 *(Revised Standard Version)* ⁵¹ *I am the living bread which came down from heaven; if any one eats of this bread, he will live forever; and the bread which I shall give for the life of the world is my flesh."*

John 6:54-56 **(R**EVISED **S**TANDARD **V**ERSION**)** ⁵⁴ *he who eats my flesh and drinks my blood has eternal life, and I will raise him up at the last day.* ⁵⁵ *For my flesh is food indeed, and my blood is drink* *indeed. ⁵⁶ He who eats my flesh and drinks my blood abides in me, and I in him.*

If you eat something that can affect your genetics; at the time of producing your seed, in it goes everything that distraught your genetics.

As far as a normal diet is concerned, I find it very interesting that there are cultures under slavery, where they always eat the same food, an example can be seen when Israel was free from Egypt, they came to the desert and they longed for the garlic and onions they ate in Egypt instead of the manna that God sent them from heaven, they preferred the food of slaves and rejected the food of angels.

This allows us to see that the Hebrews who could not be free in their way of thinking and did not change their diet of slaves for the food of God; passed this on to the next generation.

Of course, if you have a good diet, that is also what you are going to inherit to your seed, that is why you must think of yourself for the good and in an epigenetic way about your offspring.

Nutrition and Diet That Change Genetics

Longitudinal epidemiological studies have shown that there is an important association between maternal nutritional status (epigenetic effect) and the short-term presence of intrauterine growth retardation (IUGR) and in the longer term, of some chronic diseases in adults, such as cardiovascular diseases, obesity and diabetes.

Epigenetic modifications such as DNA methylation and histone modifications associated with these events have been discovered. There is evidence that these mechanisms could be the molecular bases that explain the predisposition to these diseases. By all this I am referring to the physical, but there is also a spiritual effect on what you do.

You should also consider that scientifically it has been discovered that if they change a person's physical diet, they are changing their genetics, which has an impact on a change in functions and consequently changes in destiny. The problem is that if you are changed in your functions, you may be rejecting the function that you brought from God and that will lead you to do what is not convenient or you will do things that will not be taken into account and your destiny will not be the one that God already determined.

Therefore, if you have done what was not marked by God that you should do; you have the opportunity to reposition yourself and return to do what He had destined for, how? Through the Lord's Supper, because then all your DNA is restored to its original state and is reprogrammed so that you occupy the place that corresponds to you on this earth and in the work of God, but not only will you be repositioned, but your descendants will be positioned in what they must do when they come to Earth.

All this has been scientifically been discovered through bees:

1. The Queens have longer bodies and legs than their sister workers.
2. They are thinner from their abdomens and hairless.
3. Queen bees have stingers that they can reuse when needed, unlike workers, which die after using them just once.
4. Queens can live for years, while some of their workers only live a few weeks.

5. They can also lay thousands of eggs a day; sterile worker bees tend to all royalty needs.

Given the incredible differences that exist between them, you surely think that queens are genetically different from workers.

1. The truth is that, genetically speaking, the queen is the same as the others.
2. A queen bee and her workers may come from the same parents and have identical DNA, yet their differences in behavior, physiology, and anatomy are profound.

Why?

1. Because queens eat better when they are larvae. That is what change does:
2. What they eat modifies their genetic expression, in this case through specific genes that are turned on or off, a mechanism called epigenetics.
3. When the colony decides it is time for a new queen, it picks a few lucky larvae and **bathes them in royal jelly**, a secretion rich in

protein and amino acids that is produced in glands in the mouths of young workers.
4. Initially all larvae are given a royal jelly test, but workers are quickly weaned.
5. Little princesses, however, can eat non-stop until a litter of graceful queens emerge.
6. The one who murders the rest of her royal sisters first, becomes the queen. Their genes are the same, but their genetic expression is royalty.

But no one knew why we had to wait until 2006, for the genome of the domestic bee, Apis mellifera, to be sequenced. And for 2011, for the specific details of caste differentiation to be deduced, to understand it. Like all creatures that live on this planet, bees share many genetic sequences with other animals, including humans. And researchers soon realized that one of these shared codes was for **DNA methyltransferase**, or Dnmt3, which in mammals can modify the expression of certain genes through epigenetic mechanisms.

When the researchers used chemicals to quench Dnmt3 in hundreds of larvae, they produced an entire litter of queens. When they turned it back on in another batch of larvae, they all turned into workers. More than having something additional to their workers, as you might expect, queens actually have less: apparently the royal jelly that queens eat with such enthusiasm simply dulls the gene that turns bees into workers. Of course your diet is different from the bees, (and the ingenious researchers who study it) have provided many surprising examples of the ways in which your genes express themselves to meet vital needs.

1. Then almost all of them become nurses and work together to monitor all the larval members of the honeycomb, more than a thousand times a day.
2. Later, at the advanced age of two weeks, they go out to collect nectar.
3. A team of scientists from Johns Hopkins University and Arizona State University knew that sometimes when more nurse bees are needed, the foraging bees go back to their old job, and these scientists wanted to know why; So they looked for differences in gene expression that can be found by looking for chemical "tags" that rest on certain genes; And indeed, when they compared the nurses with the

collectors, they found that in more than 150 genes those markers were in different places. So, they did an experiment: when the collectors went out to look for nectar, the researchers took all the nurses away. As soon as the collectors returned they immediately resumed their nursing duties, in no way willing to allow the young to be neglected; their pattern of genetic labels changed immediately, once they took on their new jobs.
4. Some genes that were not expressing began to do so, genes that were expressing were turned off; the foragers were not only doing a different job, they were fulfilling a different genetic destiny.

You may not look like a bee nor do feel like one, however you have a surprising amount of genetic similarities to bees, including Dnmt3. And just like those bees, gene expression can change your life suddenly, for better or for worse. Let's think about the positive because you are committed to properly feeding your life, in such a way that your offspring will be full of blessing. Maybe you already had your descendants but God can change their destiny based on what you do so that this change can take place, understanding this: consecrate yourself, congregate, serve the Lord, do good and not evil, etc.

Genetic Destiny

The pickers weren't just doing a different job; they were fulfilling a different genetic destiny.

The genetic code: Shared between bees and men is Dnmt3.

- And just like those bees, gene expression can change your life suddenly, for better or for worse as I said before.
- Whether you decide to do good or bad, this changes your genetics and genetic destiny.
- Normal larvae by eating differently; become queens.
- Pollen-gathering workers and nurses can change roles by acting differently and thus their genetics.

A Biblical example of this is seen in the following verses:

Daniel 1:3-6 *(Revised Standard Version)*
3 Then the king commanded Ash'penaz, his chief eunuch, to bring some of the people of

Israel, both of the royal family and of the nobility, ⁴ youths without blemish, handsome and skillful in all wisdom, endowed with knowledge, understanding learning, and competent to serve in the king's palace, and to teach them the letters and language of the Chalde'ans. ⁵ The king assigned them a daily portion of the rich food which the king ate, and of the wine which he drank. They were to be educated for three years, and at the end of that time they were to stand before the king. ⁶ Among these were Daniel, Hanani'ah, Mish'a-el, and Azari'ah of the tribe of Judah.

What the king of Babylon was trying to achieve was changing the genetics of these young Hebrew boys. The king knew that among their people; there were some categorized as queen bees, which meant if they reproduced they would also generate others that carried the same DNA, this was why it was the concern that they would eat Babylonian food.

Daniel 1:11-13 (revised standard version) ¹¹ Then Daniel said to the steward whom the chief of the eunuchs had appointed over Daniel, Hanani'ah, Mish'a-el, and Azari'ah, ¹² "Test your servants for ten days; let us be given vegetables to eat and water to drink. ¹³ Then let our *appearance and the appearance of the youths who eat the king's rich food be observed by you, and according to what you see deal with your servants."*

Daniel was rejecting the genetic change, but he also knew who he had trusted and that God would not leave him alone because there was faithfulness in Daniel's heart to the Lord.

The Slaves' Food

It is interesting to know that food was part of the design of a slave.

Numbers 11:5-6 *(Revised Standard Version) 5 We remember the fish we ate in Egypt for nothing, the cucumbers, the melons, the leeks, the onions, and the garlic; 6 but now our strength is dried up, and there is nothing at all but this manna to look at."*

- The food and metabolism of a slave tries to alter the BIOCHEMISTRY.
- The metabolism of an organism determines the substances that it will find nutritious and those that it will find toxic, the problem is that depending on what it may be feeding, in that it will find an appetite to

continue eating it even if it is a bad food.

Biochemical Alteration

It includes a list of all the foods that became part of the diet of the slaves in the new Land.

• Food that actually degrades the balance of the body.

Example: The food of the black race.

Studies have discovered that in the races that were subjected to slavery (African, Central American, and South American races, etc.), 80% of the diet of a person in the present has the diet of the food that their ancestors had during the days of slavery.

1. The diet of the black race to this day, is highly concentrated in vitamin K, which is good in a balanced diet, but in excess is a silent enemy of the circulation system, putting a strain on the veins and arteries.
2. These foods were overloaded with acid and destructive to the digestive system.

3. Excess vitamin K in the blood is largely responsible for so many strokes and high blood pressure that blacks suffer from.

Appetites That Affect Spiritually

Spiritually speaking, is that a believer that has not yet completely broken slavery from themselves, they then will continue to crave 80% of food from that world.

Numbers 11:5 *(Revised Standard Version)* [5] *We remember the fish we ate in Egypt for nothing, the cucumbers, the melons, the leeks, the onions, and the garlic...*

- A diet consisting of onions, garlic, cucumbers, leeks, melons, are the foods that people think they will not be able to live without; this is a type of sin that is rooted in your heart.
- This means habits, customs, traditions, appetites for things that corrupt your life.

Romans 16:18 *(Revised Standard Version)* [18] *For such persons do not serve our Lord Christ, but their own appetites,* *and by fair and flattering words they deceive the hearts of the simple-minded.*

What could be a soul's appetite? Revenge, hatred, bitterness etc. If your soul is being fed by these things, you may have a serious problem; your soul is regressing.

CHILDHOOD TRAUMAS

They can affect your genes and be epigenetic to your descendants, although they have not experienced the same trauma that you did. You are the genetic culmination of your life experiences, as well as of all the events that your parents and ancestors experienced and survived, from the happiest to the most heartbreaking.

- Also, the pills you take, the cigarettes you smoke, the drinks you drink, the exercise classes you attend and the X-rays you undergo.
- Scientists in Zurich decided to test whether early childhood trauma can affect gene expression. They did the experiment with mouse cubs, separating them from their mothers for three hours, and then returned them as blind, deaf, naked little creatures for the rest of the day.
- These findings are important because it is believed that such epigenetic

changes can persist throughout a human lifetime. This means that even if you don't remember the details of the bullying you suffered, your genes certainly do.

All this goes beyond what we can imagine, it is a difficult situation with impossible solutions unless you resort to the only and greatest divine resource that can exist; Holy Supper, because that is where you have the opportunity to restart everything that you have directly or indirectly disrupted and that has epigenetic effects. Your genes **do not forget** good or bad experiences, not even after you have gone to therapy and you feel that you overcome what you experienced with the effect of trauma because your genes register and preserve it. Before it was thought that almost all these marks or notes that were made in the genetic code, such as those that are noted in the margins of a score, **were erased before conception, but this is not the case.**

ONLY A HOLY INTERVENSION CAN ERASE THE TRAUMAS, BUT YOU NEED TO MAINTAIN YOUR FAITH IN THE POWER OF RE-GENERATION THAT ONLY THE LORD JESUS CHRIST CAN OFFER.

Child Abuse Changes Genetics

What was seen, experimented and received in childhood, has changed the genetics; for example: the women who are mistreated while pregnant will have children who will suffer with depression and are fearful and then the children of these children will carry the same problems in their genetic information, even though they may not know the complete reason of their reactions. That is, the education he received while in the womb changed his genetics. The child who sees two people of the same sex being intimate may be changing her genetics and may begin to be like them. What do you think is the mission of the education system that is teaching children about homosexuality? It is not as they say, to avoid homophobia, but the main point is to change the genetics of children.

***Luke 10:33-34 (Revised Standard Version)** 33 But a Samaritan, as he journeyed, came to where he was; and when he saw him, he had compassion, 34 and went to him and bound up his wounds, pouring on oil and wine; then he* *set him on his own beast and brought him to an inn, and took care of him.*

The word used here as wounds is (5134 trauma {trow'-mah})

TRAUMA

The Concept of hole in the SOUL is the same as a trauma: a very common concept about trauma, but interestingly it says: Trauma, from the Greek word, meaning "wound", and has the idea that it derives from the term "pierce". Thus, a TRAUMA is a wound or perforation or hole in the soul and even the human spirit.

Definitions: A hole in the soul is a perforation, any damage or injury in a part of the tripartite being (spirit, soul or body).

Multiple hole is: "Unhealed wounds and bruises in the soul cause lasting damage to a person's psychological, spiritual or emotional development and at some point produce an emotional discharge, affecting the spirit and giving rise to TRAUMA in the human spirit.

    4. MATERNAL ABUSE AND STRESS
Abuse suffered by the pregnant mother will change the unborn child's genetic. The child then is born in a sensible state of the mother even

though the child did not directly suffer the abuse.

Ezekiel 16:4 (Revised Standard Version) 4 And as for your birth, on the day you were born your navel string was not cut, nor were you washed with water to cleanse you, nor rubbed with salt, nor swathed with bands.

In the long term, it has been seen that these children have an altered response to stress, due to failures in the regulation of the hypothalamic-pituitary-adrenal (HHA) axis, in particular with alterations in autonomic responses. Recently the association between prenatal maternal depression and alterations in the HHA axis in children has also been studied, finding that a mechanism that would explain the alterations in children is the methylation of the NR3C1 gene (glucocorticoid receptor), which is sensitive to the mother's state of mind.

5. EPIGENETIC MODIFICATION BY "FVI"

In vitro embryo culture can produce epigenetic modifications. In humans, DNA methylation abnormalities associated with assisted reproductive techniques such as intracytoplasmic injection and in vitro fertilization

(IVF) have been observed. The Beckwith-Wiedemann and Angelman syndromes, produced by epigenetic alterations, have been shown to have a 3 to 6 times higher risk of occurring in children born by IVF35.

Jude 1:19 (New International Version) *¹⁹ These are the people who divide you, who follow mere natural instincts and do not have the Spirit.*

In other words, I can say it in a simpler way, that genetic manipulation can produce epigenetic damage that will bring negative consequences, both in the beginning of the genetic disruption, and in its epigenetics.

Remember that God left a process that every human being must go through, that is where He puts the human spirit from the beginning of that new life; not so when the human hand had a direct or indirect intervention.

This is true and has been scientifically discovered that from when the new life begins in the woman's womb, at this precise moment a kind of spark arises, as if it were the moment when the spirit began and human spirit began to dwell in that new life. Whatever they chose to name this process,

God is the one who decides that it is from fertilization that the human spirit arrives by divine order.

This is why when this life is being formed from its normal habitat, God does not breathe life into that new being, it can even begin to create itself according to human desires because the genetic upset is allowing many negative things in this scientific experiment to influence it but has no spirit from God.

Since one cannot live in this world without a spirit, if God does not send him, the devil fills him with an unclean spirit that was from a human that was not redeemed by God, but was recruited by darkness.

That unclean spirit may have a generic name, for example: spirit of disease, poverty, pornography, homosexuality, etc., all of these were human spirits that were not perfected and that gave them room to be unclean spirits and that the devil will use at the moment when humanity is playing god.

Genetic Transformers

1. Maternal abuse and stress.

2. In vitro Embryo culture.

3. The kind of life.

4. Poverty.

5. Emotional development.

6. Maternal behavior.

7. The environments, etc.

HOW TO BREAK EPIGENETICS?

When examining your capacity to change your future through the decisions that you make, this changes will be transmitted to future generations; for example: when one negates himself to give his tithes to God, epigenetically one is allowing for the same battles for his descendants, however when they are given with all of their heart not only is one breaking this ancestral curse but also opening the way to activate the gift of giving, activating their descendants to freely give also.

THE BREAKING OF EPIGENETICS

1 Corinthians 11:24-25 (Revised Standard Version) [24] *and when he had given thanks, he broke it, and said, "This is my body which is for you. Do this in remembrance of me."* ²⁵ *In the same way also the cup, after supper, saying, "This cup is the new covenant in my blood. Do this, as often as you drink it, in remembrance of me."*

The negative epigenetic will be broken through the participation of the bread and wine (Holy Communion). Another way of participating is in the following verse: LOVING GOD

Deuteronomy 5:9-10 (Revised Standard Version) ⁹ *you shall not bow down to them or serve them; for I the* L<small>ORD</small> *your God am a jealous God, visiting the iniquity of the fathers upon the children to the third and fourth generation of those who hate me,* ¹⁰ **but showing steadfast love to thousands of those who love me and keep my commandments.**

Another way of changing the epigenetic is loving God with all of our heart.

CONFESSION OF SINS

Leviticus 26:40-42 *(Revised Standard Version)* ⁴⁰ *"But if they confess their iniquity and the iniquity of their fathers in their treachery which they committed against me, and also in walking contrary*

to me, ⁴¹ so that I walked contrary to them and brought them into the land of their enemies; if then their uncircumcised heart is humbled and they make amends for their iniquity; ⁴² then I will remember my covenant with Jacob, and I will remember my covenant with Isaac and my covenant with Abraham, and I will remember the land.

If you confess your own iniquities and those of your parents, then God will remember the pact He made with his Son; confession of iniquity edits the negative epigenetic.

KNOWING GOD

John 8:31-36 (Revised Standard Version) *³¹ Jesus then said to the Jews who had believed in him, "If you continue in my word, you are truly my disciples, ³² and you will know the truth, and the truth will make you free." ³³ They answered him, "We are descendants of Abraham, and have never been in bondage to anyone. How is it that you say, 'You will be made free'?"³⁴ Jesus answered them, "Truly, truly, I say to you, everyone who commits sin is a slave to sin. ³⁵ The slave does not continue in the house for ever; the son continues for ever. ³⁶ So if the Son makes you free, you will be free indeed.*

Knowing the truth will change epigenetics.

WITH KNOWLEDGE

Deuteronomy 6:6 (Revised Standard Version) *⁶And these words which I command you this day shall be upon your heart...*

The instruction that the Israelites had was to repeat the law three times a day to their children, in the morning, during the day and at bedtime; with the purpose that the children would learn these laws. Certainly the parents taught these laws, however there should also be a desire in the parents and their children to learn these laws. Teaching and learning these laws with the conviction that this seed would bring a genetic change to their lives; in other words, that they could put to practice what they have learned.

LEARNING

Isaiah 1:16-18 (Revised Standard Version) *¹⁶Wash yourselves; make yourselves clean; remove the evil of your doings from before my eyes; cease to do evil, ¹⁷learn to do good; seek justice, correct oppression; defend the fatherless, plead for the widow.¹⁸ "Come now, let us reason together, says the LORD: though* *your sins are like scarlet, they shall be as white as snow; though they are red like crimson, they shall become like wool.*

Remember that the knowledge of God destroys the power of ignorance; in such a way that if ignorance is also inherited, with the knowledge of God that you seek to have in your heart; your genes will be edited and ignorance will be removed.

THE NEGATIVE LEARNING

The learning you got from your past and the negative things you have learned changed your genetics, and now you have to learn again, the positive things in order to change genetics again. If you don't learn the good again; you will not change and you will always continue to do the same. The problems and the battles will be the same and you will lose again.

THE CEREBRAL PROCESS OF LEARNING

Every time you evoke a memory or mentally analyze information you erase the previous synaptic network and record a new one in its place, reaffirming certain aspects of the information, weakening others, and / or adding new data to the neural network. This means that every moment that passes, your brain changes and is literally different from how it was in the previous moment.

This means that the teacher or professor of the XXI century, must learn to work the epigenome of their students in order to obtain a better learning.

http://www.redem.org/como-se-relaciona-la-epigenetica-con-el-aprendizaje/

How then does one work on the epigenome of students?

Achieving greater psychological knowledge of the student in person (conversations, scheduled interviews for each student at set times and also online). Learn about the negative and positive aspects of the life of each student, that is, their weaknesses and strengths. Every teacher must be a counselor and researcher (face-to-face and online).

That is why it is very important that you manage to assimilate everything that I am leaving embodied in this book, with the purpose that you have the opportunity to edit your epigenetics and that you can evolve to your original state to the moment when God created you, but you commit to learning all that this warrants.

OTHER WAYS OF BREAKING INHERITED EPIGENETICS

Being Filled with The Holy Spirit

Matthew 1:18-20 (Revised Standard Version) *[18] Now the birth of Jesus Christ took place in this way. When his mother Mary had been betrothed to Joseph, before they came together she was found to be with child of the Holy Spirit; [19] and her husband Joseph, being a just man and unwilling to put her to shame, resolved to divorce her quietly. [20] But as he considered this, behold, an angel of the Lord appeared to him in a dream, saying, "Joseph, son of David, do not fear to take Mary your wife, for that which is conceived in her is of the Holy Spirit...*

BY THE MINISTRATION AND DELIVERANCE OF THE SOUL

Ezekiel 16:4 (Revised Standard Version) *[4] And as for your birth, on the day you were born your navel string was not cut, nor were you washed with water to cleanse you, nor rubbed with salt, nor swathed with bands.*

All of this in order to reach the following:

THE NEW RACE

2 Corinthians 5:17 (Revised Standard Version) *[17] Therefore, if anyone is in Christ, he is a **new creation;** the old has passed away, behold, the new has come.*

It is necessary that you can make an examination of your interior with the purpose that you see the need for a change in your life, being conscious that you must start from your DNA with the editing of your genetics. You may not be able to completely understand it, but if you prepare your life for the change you need; wherever you are, God will see your heart's longing to achieve the radical change you need in your DNA and He will do whatever it takes for you to be fully restored.

Chapter 6
The Receptors Of The Generational Spirit

It is necessary to assimilate the ideas and concepts of all these topics that we have been teaching in order for the following verse to come to pass:

John 8:32 (Revised Standard Version) *³² and you will know the truth, and the truth will make you free."*

This shows us that according to the knowledge one acquires, that person will break certain limitations, with this new knowledge you will experience greater levels of deliverance each time, nobody can say they do not desire another level of freedom because there will always be something new to learn on the topic.

Remember that the deception that occurred at some point by darkness, was not what the enemy intended to leave halfway done nor did the enemy think that it would simply weaken you; The attack of the enemy was with the purpose of destroying you completely starting with the spirit, soul until reaching the body, achieving this through transgressions, sins and iniquities.

1 John 3:8 (Revised Standard Version) *⁸ He who commits sin is of the devil; for the devil has sinned from the beginning. The reason the Son of God* *appeared was to destroy the **works of the devil.***

The only one who can undo everything that the enemy has been doing against you, is Jesus, why do I ask? Because when you investigate what the word **WORKS** means, it clearly shows that it is an act that is done until it is completed.

It started from the most insignificant, you can see an example in the construction of a building; maybe no one sees how it all started, but the first thing they did was clean the land, remove anything that could get in their way. The devil does the same, he takes away those good things that you have, so that there is no hindrance in the destruction he is carrying out, he brings havoc against the foundations to manipulate you at will.

As you have read in 1 John 3:8; Jesus came to destroy the works of the enemy. Jesus began with the not visible until reaching all that was visible. Because when God begins a work it is taken seriously until completed. This is why it is important to learn about our ancestors in order to know how to battle against our genetic influence, this is a strong battle that is as strong as fighting with the devil himself.

For this reason, when you hear about the battle against darkness, some people will be afraid, this is an invisible kingdom that cannot be seen with natural eyesight but is very real. This is why it is critical to be cautious because one of the biggest goals of the enemy is to demonize people. There are demons that affect families, health, economy, emotions etc. In such a way that when someone who has suffered from all of this hears about spiritual warfare, they shudder.

But then, you should know that in the same way as the battles are strong in the spiritual, the battle in the genetics is equal or worse, although people do not consider it that way. That is why it is necessary that you be open-minded by being properly warned, you can learn what to do to get up and fight properly and counteract such attacks; considering then that genetics plays a very important role in your life and that at the same time it will let you see the power of that genetic influence.

Based on what God has allowed me to see in the course of my life of the spiritual world of darkness;

An obscure world with entities that belong to realm realm may be more aware of their influence than a believer can have. These entities can genetically speaking exert an attack to the genetics to achieve a great damage.

Demons or unclean spirits cannot suffer a genetic influence because they do not have blood but they know that this type of influence has devastating effects once they manage to alter the genes in someone.

That is why within everything that makes up darkness, there is a spirit acting as the main spirit in charge of moving everything that is involved in the genetic disruption, although it is a generic name, it can have a lot of influence for what it does, I am referring to the generational spirit; This in turn is assigned the job of identifying the spirit that is assigned to pursue the genetic data of each person and that when finding a negative data it will do everything possible por each person to be presented with different scenarios where they will fall into different temptations that the adversary will launch at them.

This generational spirit not only will it track the genetic code but it will also manipulate it; in order to completely overcome a person's live in these situations. This continues to occur until there is divine intervention from God, here is where an opportunity to break every curse against

God's children emerges. I also want to mention that it is also very difficult to triumph from these attacks without God's intervention.

Receptors

Hence, the need arises to explain as explicitly as possible what refers to the recipients of generational spirits, with the assurance that God is promoting this material. Reaching this knowledge has been a supernatural experience; but even more extraordinary is His love because despite everything, He is sending the revelation that will lead His people to true and total freedom.

In other words, there is an attack that has filtered into the essence that makes up your person as a human being; that essence is your DNA which, when being disrupted by the darkness.

This can open doors that will allow sickness to be added to someone's genes that will then operate against that person; seeking their destruction. Not only of your life affected but also of your future generations, because those diseases that you may be acquiring today may not finish developing in your person, however when you inherit it from your descendants, it will be activated in any of them at the least moment thought-out.

How then does the receptor operation work? The Bible mentions many verses that what contaminates is what comes out of a person.

Mark 7:20-23 (Revised Standard Version) *[20] And he said, "What comes out of a man is what defiles a man. [21] For from within, out of the heart of man, come evil thoughts, fornication, theft, murder, adultery, [22] coveting, wickedness, deceit, licentiousness, envy, slander, pride, foolishness. [23] All these evil things come from within, and they defile a man."*

- There is no doubt that these are what are called RECEIVERS ...
- And they were once placed in the life of the BELIEVER and if it is still there those same are the ones that will attract the influence of spirits of high places

TECHNICAL CONCEPT OF RECEIVERS:

In order to understand the dynamics of a spiritual receptor, we need to use the technical concept, for example:

Receptors: the areas that spirits most frequently stalk AND AFFECT within the soul or body of a person, this is due to the fact that there is something that attracts them and that functions as receptors. Technical concept: A device that receives signals. Examples: television, radio, cable. The receivers of the devil: They are for the purpose of polluting and if possible killing of the person.

Receptor's dynamics:

TRANSMITTER: A spirit that sends influence signals in the environment.

RECEPTOR: It is something inside a person that has the ability or probability to be influenced by a spirit.

Capacities: laws, rights, ancestors amplifying the signal.

TIMES OF CONTAMINATION WITH RECEIVERS:

#1 Ancestors: A level of iniquity is reached when a spirit is contaminated thus allowing this contamination will allow these receptors to be transferred to our descendants. Exodus 20:4-6.

#2 Childhood: The environment in which we participate will allow for the receivers one will acquire. 2 Samuel 4:4.

2 Samuel 4:4 (Revised Standard Version) *⁴Jonathan, the son of Saul, had a son who was crippled in his feet. He was five years old when the news about Saul and Jonathan came from Jezreel; and his nurse took him up, and fled; and, as she fled in her haste, he fell, and became lame. And his name was Mephib'osheth.*

#3 The life we lived in the world without Christ:

Ephesians 2:1-2 (Revised Standard Version) *And you he made alive, when you were dead through the trespasses and sins 2 in which you once walked, following the course of this world, following the prince of the power of the air, the spirit that is now at work in the sons of disobedience.*

The search for receivers:

Spirit that pursues signals emitted by receptor. The emitting spirit operates in the body, soul, spirit and DNA of a person. GENERATIONAL spirit visits generations and has arrived through a generational breach.

- Then when the generational spirit finds the receiver that is operating it then will hide in a person's DNA.
- It is like an insect that attacks a tree during its different stages in order to affect its fruit and the nature of the tree.

THE DYNAMICS BETWEEN THE RECEPTOR AND TRANSMITTOR:

If negative ancestors are not broken, the generational spirit will return because its nature is cyclical and its assignment is to visit the generations of each bloodline ...

(Luke 11:24-26 RSV) *²⁴"When the unclean spirit has gone out of a man, he passes through waterless places seeking rest; and finding none he says, 'I will return to my <u>house</u> from which I came.' ²⁵ And when he comes he finds it swept and put in order. ²⁶ Then he goes and brings seven other spirits more evil than himself, and they enter and dwell there; and the last state of that man becomes worse than the first."*

<u>House:</u> OIKOS #3624 meaning, house, room, tabernacle.

- Another member of the family
- When it decides to return to the home from where it left, it can also refer to a home where other members of the same family may be living.

Without Receivers inside: When the sent message does not find a receiver, the transmission is aborted without actually fulfilling the enemy's mission.

John 14:30 (RSV) *30 I will no longer talk much with you, for the ruler of this world is coming. He has no power over me...*

SUPERVISION TIME:

Every believer will have the opportunity of a supervision that God makes gives us through his spirit in order to see if we are working on reducing the levels of iniquity inherited from our ancestors, before the TRANSMITTING spirit of darkness comes to look for the receivers of iniquity.

1. God visits to supervise and see if we are working on reducing these levels.

2. Spirits of high places seek receivers.

VISITORS OF 2 SPIRITUAL REALMS

When God visits: (Deut 5:9) ⁹you shall not bow down to them or serve them; for I the LORD your God am a jealous God, visiting the iniquity of the fathers upon the children to the third and fourth generation of those who hate me,

When a generational spirit visits:

***2 Samuel 12:4** ⁴Now there came a traveler to the rich man, and he was unwilling to take one of his own flock or herd to prepare for the wayfarer who had come to him, but he took the poor man's lamb, and prepared it for the man who had come to him."*

David's genetic ghost: What parents decide to do affects their children...

1. 10 generations before David's lineage: Another named Tamar involved with incest (Genesis 38:13-18)
2. David's sexual problems (2 Samuel 12)
3. The sexual problems of the sons: Absalom violated his concubines; Salomon had 1000 women; Amnon raped his sister Tamar (2 Samuel 13:10-15)

One of the truths that we can learn in the bible is the meaning of "The long-term impact of family havoc." **Why does the generational spirit visit the genes?** Because all of this is a product of a divine engineer, God is the one that created humanity with genetic data, because he is a generational God, familial; this is why when God presents himself, He is Father, Son and Holy Spirit. Someone could ask, "where is the mother in all this?" because she is necessary for a family unit, to this I want to say the following; the Holy Spirit without being a feminine entity, speaking mystically, has motherly functions, just as consoling and convicting.

Hence the family figure, just as in humanity. God designed the family to consist of father, mother, sons and daughters; thus forming a kind of photograph on the human plane, which speaks of our God as a familiar God.

In such a way that genetic engineering is a design of God, which is why He is a generational God and that will always move with humanity, through generations. You can see that in the Old Testament, God called a man, made a covenant with him, and gives him promises; but the greatest thing is that the promise is fulfilled by saying that He is the God of Abraham, Isaac and Jacob; that is extremely interesting because then there is generational and genealogical data in His word.

Psalms 90:1-2 (RSV) *Lord, thou hast been our dwelling place in all generations. ² Before the mountains were brought forth, or ever thou hadst formed the earth and the world, from everlasting to everlasting thou art God.*

When it says from generation to generation, it may be seen as generations; therefore He is God of generations. The interesting thing is that before all creation, He was already refuge to the generations that would one day exist. Of course this is based on the idea of pre-existence.

On the other hand, you must also remember that the origin of the word generations is, GENE, from which the word genetics, genealogy, generations and many more that come from the term GENE is also derived. This is not a mere simple idea or a single word but Gene is something inside of you that makes up a kind of folder with stored data, generational codes that have been compiled through the lives of your ancestors; which becomes a kind of general file with several folders where depending on the information will also be the gene, this is, the folder has different information stored and that will suddenly be evident by what it contains. That is why you come to be the result of the sum of your ancestors.

Genesis 3:15 (NIV) [15] God also said to Moses, "Say to the Israelites, 'The Lord, the God of your fathers—the God of Abraham, the God of Isaac and the God of Jacob—has sent me to you.' "This is my name forever, the name you shall call me from **generation to generation.**

This is the second Bible verse I mention to let you see that He is a God of generations. Maybe your ancestors did not have the necessary discernment to hear God's voice, but now you are the blessed one that receives the revelation to discern when God is speaking, in order to discern the times. To know what to do in different situations, this is a great blessing with which you are editing your genes and in the respective folder saving the information that your ancestors wrongly wrote.

Today you are editing and filing in your genes in order for your descendants to have a better life; and through this divine intervention you can break ancestral curses I order to have an opportunity of a new beginning.

God Designed Us with Dna

That is why genetic engineering, although it uses human terms, is a matter of divine character as I have already mentioned throughout this book; in such a way that the only one with the ability to create human DNA is God.

Psalms 145:4 (NIV) *4 One generation commends your works to another; they tell of your mighty acts.*

God is the main engineer of the genetic design, and one of the reasons why He designed you this way was so that man would have God's information with the purpose of when generating that information it would be transmitted through the sperm to the woman's womb and that when she gave birth, the child would have God's design and in turn, when the child multiplied, he would transfer what is of God because that was what his genes had.

Or as I have already exemplified in a more didactic way, perhaps, their folders had the information that the Lord had left in each one; documents written by the hand of God and deposited in each gene.

But the point is that when multiplied to the next generation, his genes would be according to divine design. Unfortunately the information has been disrupted by the enemy with the fall of the first man.

Psalms 145:4 (NIV) *4 One generation commends your works to another; they tell of your mighty acts.*

Thank God there is a divine intervention where the hand of God arrives to edit what is written in each folder, in all of your genes that are still in you. This with the purpose that you reach a new opportunity in your generation and the future generations that come out of your loins, that they celebrate the wonderful works that only God can do because He is the main engineer in the design of all your DNA.

I say all this because humanity is not the product of God's pastime or the evolution of a monkey to become a man. Humanity is the product of God's engineering, of the mind of the Lord, where no one can go to manipulate anything; He took the time to do the wonders of which today you have in your entire tripartite being: spirit, soul and body.

For this reason, humanity is the crown of creation, from the moment God placed him in the garden. He first created all that you see around you and lastly he crowned creation with humanity. God appropriately designed DNA in order to transfer genes and form generations and generations.

You really do not live only for yourself, but you are the bridge of blessing that God wants to use to form new generations, precisely through the genes rewriting all His information and that it is then said: these people are from God, because they come from another group who decided to allow God to edit all their information that was in their genes which was disrupted by the enemy.

What is remembered and the Bible itself testifies is that there was a people that God took for himself, he took them from a man who came from pagan people, but God called him and he put revelation in Abraham so that they would know who God was and Israel came from there. These people are known throughout the world as the people of God. You know the history; From the moment when they rejected Jesus, the opportunity was opened for you to become part of the spiritual Israel of God, the Church of the Lord Jesus Christ made up of everyone who recognizes Jesus as their Lord and Savior. That is where a very great miracle arises because being pagans, no matter who it was, would have the opportunity to be part of what today are known as God's people.

Hence the importance of understanding that there is a genetic design, you cannot deny that you live for yourself only, but for your next generation; in such a way that if the design was disrupted, although it is true that you continue to function with an apparent normality; when the moment of natural multiplication arrives, the damage that has been suffered in genetics is transferred there also. Obviously, all the genetics that God put into you is passed down but if you have suffered a genetic alteration this will also pass to the next generation.

That is why there is a phrase that is very frequently heard that says that people were born in a certain religion and thus will die with that religion, because that is what they received, it was a religious inheritance of idolatry that borders on ignorance, but the disruption was such that many prefer to follow in their error, without thinking that in them is the opportunity for their descendants may no longer come with the same problem.

In you is the opportunity, of the original design that God made may be returned to you; but you will only achieve it as far as you allow it; because in reality when that design was developed, its human effect was to do the will of God, man's desires were those of God, he persevered in God's call, praise and adoration was according to what the Lord likes, etc., but when the enemy's deception attack came, a gap was opened so that the negative information began to damage the positive and multiply, to the point that when there is a new multiplication, the structure is the same but contaminated and moves but only the negative.

When I speak of contamination and negative things, I mean what is manifested in the character, for example: disobedient parents, equally disobedient children; in such a way that nothing different can be expected in their children because it is influenced by the genetic code that their parents inherited. I only mention this as a reminder because I have already mentioned it in the previous chapters.

Transferable Engineering

Psalms 78:1-8 *Give ear, O my people, to my teaching; incline your ears to the words of my mouth!* ²*I will open my mouth in a parable; I will utter dark sayings from of old,* ³*things that we have heard and known, that our fathers have told us.* ⁴*We will not hide them from their children, but tell to the coming generation the glorious deeds of the* LORD, *and his might, and the wonders which he has wrought.* ⁵*He established a testimony in Jacob, and appointed a law in Israel, which he commanded our fathers to teach to their children;* ⁶*that the next generation might know them, the children yet unborn, and arise and tell them to their children,* ⁷*so that they should set their hope in God, and not forget the works of God, but keep his commandments;* ⁸*and that they should not be like their fathers, a stubborn and rebellious generation, a generation whose heart was not steadfast, whose spirit was not faithful to God.*

With this verse you can see that God gave Israel commandments and bylaws to give to their children, and they to their own children, with the purpose of teaching all to place their trust in God and to not forget they belonged to God; with this you can also see that for every generation God a time of visitation; with the purpose of each generation having an opportunity to change their genetics.

In fact, the opportunity that you have to be equipped through this book is because God has allowed the veil to be removed and for you to reach the necessary knowledge so that can you find the restoration of your DNA with the purpose of breaking those attacks, otherwise the disruption is increasingly degenerative because the inheritance that is received is like a fuel to sinfully activate the life of a person, but then it is not only his inheritance, but that person contributes with his own life to that this genetic disruption grows and that their descendants receive the inheritance increasingly stronger in the negative.

This is why you must consider Daniel's prayer, it was not a religious prayer because he had some knowledge about this topic, being that he repented for the sins of his parents:

Daniel 9:4-6 (RSV) *⁴I prayed to the L͞ORD my God and made confession, saying, "O Lord, the great and terrible God, who keeps covenant and steadfast love with those who love him and keep his commandments, ⁵we have sinned and* *done wrong and acted wickedly and rebelled, turning aside from thy commandments and ordinances; [6] we have not listened to thy servants the prophets, who spoke in thy name to our kings, our princes, and our fathers, and to all the people of the land.*

Daniel would pray with knowledge not mere words, he prayed asking for forgiveness from the depth of his heart because he knew that his parents' sins were within him. Daniel was aware that if he did not put a stop to these sins, the next generation would have greater problems and they would offend God in a greater way.

Now the problem is that possibly you have never gotten to pray that way because you do not feel the indignation or shame of the iniquity that you carry inside and the effect that it can cause in the future of others. Of course that includes me but I am referring to your person because my purpose is to make you aware of all this so that you rise up as a warrior of light in the name of Jesus and you can purify your life for the benefit of yourself and your descendants.

Remember that to all this, you must add that the devil has a diagram of the weak areas of your life and has the strategy of darkness to launch his attack to knock you down, he does not do it to see if he can weaken you, but that ancestral sin may come to life by empowering it becomes more difficult to uproot in subsequent generations. Remember that if you are the sum of your ancestors, tomorrow you will be the sum to your children and so on.

That is why it is very important to be aware of all this with the purpose that a spirit of repentance descends on your life and you cry out to God so that your genetics have a total reset and see sin as something that can be overcome or dominated at any time. In order to have that revelation, it is necessary that repentance enter the heart. You must consider that if the genes are not transferred properly by your ancestors, the descendants become people without dreams of God in their lives.

It is clear that I do not intend to point out or accuse anyone, what I want is that you can reflect on the operation of error that the enemy has had against God's children, which I must also take into account that I also have ancestors and descendants of my own, therefore you and I have the opportunity for a radical change for the next generations. For this to happen, it is necessary to work on renouncing the force of inherited iniquity and as a result you can then lead your descendants to a different story through a complete submission to God, going through a deliverance and breaking ancestral chains so that your inheritance is a blessing, an inheritance totally edited for good.

This is where what I have already explained about the Golgi apparatus comes into play, which is like a cell and is responsible for transmitting information to DNA through proteins. The interesting thing is that DNA had been designed to receive and transfer only good things and reject the bad, but after a deception, the DNA receives contamination in the form of protein, accepts it and deliberately begins to undergo negative changes because the protein has a disruption that when it begins to function as it should, the evil embedded there is unpacked and the DNA becomes disrupted.

I described this in detail in the previous chapters, but I am very interested that you can keep it in mind as of today, as it remains relevant it will also push you to seek total restoration.

The Golgi apparatus is like a transport of evil, it is in charge of taking everything that is harmful in a stem cell and transfer it to those that will inherit it and there is a sequence of evil from generation to generation, to then close the doors to the Word of God. Although if someone knows that they have problems that are incomprehensible to their logic, they can ask the following question: how did the alcoholism problems come if I never drank?

When this understanding arrives, the person will be willing to go through the necessary in order for their soul to be delivered.

But you must also know that this is the product of God's mercy, this revelation He sends at this time is because it is the end times and the Lord wants you to be perfected, but for that, you need to have the knowledge so that you can do what is possible and God will do the impossible.

Another important point I want to highlight here, is

that Golgi, originally was in charge of transmitting positive information from generation to generation, however, at the fall of man it was disrupted and now it only transmits iniquity; that is why deliverance is vital, through the power of the blood of Christ.

In other words, Golgi has always been a means of transportation, but it had a reprogramming from the positive to the negative. From here I can understand then that the basis of your redemption is with blood, but it is not just any blood because there is no greater power in terms of blood, than the blood of the Lamb of God, the blood that Jesus shed on the cross in Calvary. This was so that, once you have believed in Him, you can have the opportunity to be totally restored until being brought to the original state as you came from the hand of God.

CONCEPTION

At conception, the sperm carries the iniquity in the form of protein through each globule, it fertilizes the egg and transfers the influence to the child, so that when the child grows up he behaves like his father, who resembles the grandfather with everything even the same illnesses that his great-grandfather had. That is why God visits the generations with the purpose of seeing if those who have had generational problems are in search of restoration or deliberately adjust themselves to see how their generations are destroyed.

Genetic Battle

Ezekiel 16:3-4 (RSV) *³and say, Thus says the Lord GOD to Jerusalem: Your origin and your birth are of the land of the Canaanites; your father was an Amorite, and your mother a Hittite. ⁴And as for your birth, on the day you were born your navel string was not cut, nor were you washed with water to cleanse you, nor rubbed with salt, nor swathed with bands.*

According to this verse, you can see that God is speaking to Israel, He tells them that they were from descendants of Canaan and observe what God says about their parents; they were people that were once enemies of God's people. This was why Israel continuously fell in the same sin of idolatry; because of the genetic influence that was in their DNA. That is why it says that the umbilical cord was not cut, because he continued with the same customs from his idolatrous influence. Breaking the umbilical cord is breaking with genetic influence, both biological and spiritual.

GENERATIONAL SPIRIT

This spirit visits generations and first arrived through a generational breach. It operates and hides in DNA of a person.

When God spoke to Israel, he presented to them by using an insect as a figure, for example: insects attack trees, crops, sows and the cultivation of crops.

What God has allowed me to teach for many years is that the genealogy tree in order to explain the origin of each person, of course this is not something I invented, but scientists in anthropology teach us where the person comes from under the same concept of what is a family tree.

FAMILY TREE OF 14 PEOPLE

- It is a picture of the filiation of a family, represented by a tree.
- Shows the series of ancestors of each individual (Lineage).

When God spoke of an insect to understand the attack on the generations he put the tree also, observe its phases:

1. Fruits: enjoy 4th.

Generation = Grandchildren

2. Branches and Leaves: 3rd beauty.

Generation = CHILDREN

3. Trunk: strength, vigor 2nd.

Generation = PARENTS

Los Ancestros

4. Root: 1st inheritance.

Generation = GRANDPARENTS

Another point that I have had the opportunity to teach before is that you are the fifteen in your ancestral line of fourteen people, in other words, three generations made up of eight great-grandparents, four grandparents and two parents.

The information that you carry inside is primary but as I taught in the previous chapters, the information that you carry inside, extends to more people, that is 42 people who contributed so that you carry in your DNA the information of everything they did throughout their lives, both good and bad.

But to understand the depth of our battle we will only take the biblical example of four generations that is fourteen people

Joel 1:4 (RSV) *4 What the cutting locust left, the swarming locust has eaten. What the swarming locust left, the hopping locust has eaten, and what the hopping locust left, the destroying locust has eaten.*

It is the same insect although in different stages, it is a small insect at the beginning then finally becomes a locust, but initially attacks the root, trunk, branch and finally the fruits. This is the attack of the generational spirit in different stages why it is necessary that you know where and / or for what reason an attack can come; I will also show you the history of biblical people who had the generational influence, which made them have a future as the Bible shows us.

THE ANCESTORS OF "THE HERODS"

1. In them you can see how the ancestral inheritance angles operated.
2. Generational spirit, generational curses and generational flaws.
3. This is a clear example of the power of the ancestors.

THE STORY OF THE SPIRIT OF HEROD

1. The first Herod was called, "Herod the Great.
    a. He built a temple for the Jews
    b. He tried to kill Jesus when he was a child
2. The second Herod, "Herod Archelaus."
3. The third Herod, "Herod Antipas or the tetrarch"

a. He committed adultery with his brother's wife.
   b. He killed John the Baptist.
4. The fourth Herod, "Herod Agrippa"
   a. This was the one to whom the Apostle Paul preached to.
5. The fifth Herod, "Herodias"

6. The sixth Herod, "Bernice"

7. Sister of Herod Agrippa.

8. The seventh Herod, "Herod the king"
   a. He instituted the persecution of the church.
   b. He killed the first apostle.

THE FOURTH HERODIAN GENERATION

To the fourth Herod, Herod Agrippa, Paul presents Christ as his savior to which Herod almost became a Christian:

Acts 26:27-29 (RSV) *²⁷King Agrippa, do you believe the prophets? I know that you* believe." ²⁸ And Agrippa said to Paul, "In a short time you think to make me a Christian!" ²⁹ And Paul said, "Whether short or long, I would to God that not only you but also all who hear me this day might become such as I am—except for these chains."

1. The fourth Herod as a symbol of the fourth generation, had the opportunity to change family history but instead rejected the opportunity. Remember that the fourth generation is the present and is given the opportunity to change the destiny of future generations.

Exodus 34:7 (RSV) *⁷ keeping steadfast love for thousands, forgiving iniquity and transgression and sin, but who will by no means clear the guilty, visiting the iniquity of the fathers upon the children and the children's children, to the third and the fourth generation."*

Exodus 20:5 (RSV)*⁵ you shall not bow down to them or serve them; for I the LORD your God am a jealous God, visiting the iniquity of the fathers upon the children to the third and the fourth generation of those who hate me...*

Numbers 14:18 (RSV) *¹⁸ 'The LORD is slow to anger, and abounding in steadfast* *love, forgiving iniquity and transgression, but he will by no means clear the guilty, visiting the iniquity of fathers upon children, upon the third and upon the fourth generation.'*

Deuteronomy 5:9 (RSV) *⁹ you shall not bow down to them or serve them; for I the LORD your God am a jealous God, visiting the iniquity of the fathers upon the children to the third and fourth generation of those who hate me,*

With Herod's ancestors you can see how this situation worked in the ancestral line of that family. Now I want to show you a more recent dynasty:

KENNEDY'S ANCESTORS

Joseph Kennedy Sr.- his dream was that all his children became politicians.

1. The highest or main importer of liquor licensed in the United States of America.

2. He was the first authorized man to bring rum and gin to this very nation.

3. The curse started by introducing liquor into his generation.

4. The Bible speaks against those who lead people to get drunk.

Habakkuk 2:15-16 (RSV) *¹⁵ Woe to him who makes his neighbors drink of the cup of his wrath, and makes them drunk, to gaze on their shame! ¹⁶ You will be sated with contempt instead of glory. Drink, yourself, and stagger! The cup in the* LORD'S *right hand will come around to you, and shame will come upon your glory!*

First generation

Joseph Kennedy Jr. (Anti-Semitism) - died in 1944 in a plane crash.

> 1. He called the Jews an detestable specimen of man.

> 2. What Hitler had done was the best thing against the Jews, according to this character.

> 3. He said that we should be envious of what Hitler did to the Jews.

> 4. That statement was made from Germany 1934.

Genesis 12:3 (RSV) *³I will bless those who bless you, and him who curses you I will curse; and by you all the families of the earth shall bless themselves.*

John F. Kennedy- was assassinated on November 22, 1963 in Dallas, Texas. The next born son of Joseph Kennedy became the first catholic president of the United State of America.

Exodus 20:4-5 (RSV) ⁴"You shall not make for yourself a graven image, or any likeness of anything that is in heaven above, or that is in the earth beneath, or that is in the water under the earth;

⁵you shall not bow down to them or serve them; for I the LORD your God am a jealous God, visiting the iniquity of the fathers upon the children to the third and the fourth generation of those who hate me...

Kathleen Kennedy

1. Became a widow after only being married four months, then died in France on May 13, 1948 in a plane crash with her lover. This was also the year that Israel was recognized as a nation.

Exodus 20:5 (RSV) *⁵you shall not bow down to them or serve them; for I the* LORD *your God am a jealous God, visiting the iniquity of the fathers upon the children to the third and the fourth generation of those who hate me...*

Robert Kennedy- dies June 6, 1968, on the anniversary of the six days of war between Israel and Jordan.

1. He was shot and wounded on June 5, 1968 at 12:03 pm. In the hallway that led from the main living room to the kitchen of the Ambassador Hotel in Los Angeles California. A Palestinian man, Iver Johnson had a 22 caliber revolver in his hands and shot Robert Kennedy six times.

John F. Kennedy Jr.- In 1999 dies in an arial accident.

1. According to studies, the span of an American life is of seventy years.
2. In the Kennedy family the average lifespan of those who died was only forty-four years.

Edward M. Kennedy- Dies in the year 2009.

He survives a plane crash, he was also in a car accident in 1969.

ANCESTORS OF ISRAELITE PATRIARCHS

1. Genesis 12: 10-20 Abraham lied about his wife Sarah.

2. Genesis 26: 6-11 Isaac lied about his wife Rebekah.

3. Genesis 27: 1-25 Jacob lied to his father saying he was Esau.

4. Genesis 37 Eleven sons of Jacob kept the lie a secret for seventeen years, regarding Joseph.

5. Genesis 46:34 Joseph's lie, influenced his brothers to say that they were cattlemen and not shepherds.

DAVID'S ANCESTORS

The generational law meant that whatever parents did, this would affect their children until they rise to break this influence over their lives.

Exodus 20:5 (RSV) *⁵you shall not bow down to them or serve them; for I the LORD your God am a jealous God, visiting the iniquity of the fathers upon the children to* *the third and the fourth generation of those who hate me...*

Some example:

1. David's problems.
2. Sexual = adultery and fornication.
3. Your children's problems.
4. Absalom raped concubines.
5. Solomon had 1000 wives.
6. Amnon raped his sister Tamar (2 Samuel 13: 10- 15).
7. Ten generations earlier in the line of David.
8. Another Tamar involved with Judah in a type of incest (Genesis 38: 13-18).

A spirit that starts from an individual, will try to return to the house or to the descendants of his family. This is a generational spirit that is familiar with family members.

CYCLES OF GENERATIONAL SPIRITS

If negative ancestors are not broken, the generational spirit will return because it is cyclical and its task is to visit generations of each bloodline.

Luke 11:24-26 (RSV) [24] *"When the unclean spirit has gone out of a man, he passes through waterless places seeking* rest; and finding none he says, 'I will return to my house from which I came.' ²⁵ And when he comes he finds it swept and put in order. ²⁶ Then he goes and brings seven other spirits more evil than himself, and they enter and dwell there; and the last state of that man becomes worse than the first."

House: OIKOS #3624 meaning, house, room, tabernacle.

1. Another member of the family; by saying:... I will return to the house where I came from... it can also refer to the house where there are other members of the same family.

7 TYPES OF GENERATIONAL SPIRITS:

The most common in families:

1. Anger (1 Samuel 18:8)

2. Fear (18:12)

3. Jealousy (18: 9)

4. Manipulation (18: 12-30)

5. Death (18:11)

6. Witchcraft (28: 3-25)

7. Suicide (31:4)

In the house (family) of Saul, there were some of these 7 generational spirits; they affected Saul, Jonathan (death), Michal (jealousy), Mephibosheth (fear).

A legal right (spiritually speaking): In a born again, hell is no longer the problem, but the entanglements of life.

1. The Bible shows that the sin of unrepentant parents leads their generations to be bearers of negative effects.

It is my desire that the content of this book takes you to a spiritual level of a warrior of light and that you can rise up in the name of Jesus and fight to rid yourself of any contamination that may be in your DNA, in order to take advantage of all the blessings that the Lord has in store for you, but also to prepare the ground for your descendants.

www.ingramcontent.com/pod-product-compliance
Lightning Source LLC
Chambersburg PA
CBHW070532170426
43200CB00011B/2402